EMPERORS DO:

Very few of the Roman emperors died a natural death. The insane
Caligula was murdered after leaving the theatre; Caracalla while he
was relieving himself. Caesar was stabbed twenty-three times and
Otho was dragged into the Tiber with a flesh-hook. However great
an emperor's power, danger was ever present.

This fresh and engaging book looks at each of the Roman emperors from Julius Caesar in 44 BC to Romulus Augustulus in
AD 476, illuminating not only the manner of their deaths but what
their final days tell us about their lives. We also hear how the most
powerful position in the history of the Western world held a permanent appeal, despite its perils, with eager candidates constantly
coming forward to seize the throne.

Emperors Don't Die in Bed provides a clear history of the imperial
succession as well as a compelling depiction of the intrigue and
drama of Roman imperial politics.

Fik Meijer is Professor of Ancient History at the University of
Amsterdam.

EMPERORS DON'T DIE IN BED

Fik Meijer

Translated by S.J. Leinbach

Routledge
Taylor & Francis Group

LONDON AND NEW YORK

First published 2001
by Athenaeum–Polak & Van Gennep
Singel 262, NL-1016 AC Amsterdam

First published in English 2004
by Routledge
11 New Fetter Lane, London EC4P 4EE

Simultaneously published in the USA and Canada
by Routledge
29 West 35th Street, New York, NY 10001

Routledge is an imprint of the Taylor & Francis Group
© Fik Meijer, 2001
Translation © Routledge, 2004

Typeset in 11/12pt Garamond 3 by Graphicraft Limited, Hong Kong
Printed and bound in Great Britain by MPG Books Ltd, Bodmin

This publication has been made possible with the financial
support from the Foundation for the Production and
Translation of Dutch Literature.

British Library Cataloguing in Publication Data
A catalogue record for this book is available from
the British Library

Library of Congress Cataloging in Publication Data
A Catalog record for this book has been requested

ISBN 0-415-31201-9 (hbk)
ISBN 0-415-31202-7 (pbk)

CONTENTS

CONTENTS

INTRODUCTION

The history of the Roman Empire officially starts in 27 BC, but the history of Rome begins much earlier, in 753 BC. In that year, according to tradition, the twin brothers Romulus and Remus established a small settlement on the left bank of the Tiber. In seven centuries Rome grew from a city-state in central Italy to the dazzling centre of an immense empire. This growth began shortly after the city was founded. In the Regal Period (753–509 BC) the small community on the Tiber developed into a real city, which would become the political, economic and cultural centre of the region. The long rule of the Etruscan kings unquestionably stimulated the urbanisation of Rome. It was they who drained and paved the low-lying, centrally located plain between the Capitol in the west, the Palatine in the south and the Quirinal in the north, thus creating the *Forum Romanum*, the political heart of Rome.

In 509 BC the last king, the Etruscan Tarquinius Superbus, was deposed by the Roman aristocrats, an event that marked the start of the Republic, a form of government that would endure for almost five centuries. The leadership was in the hands of the Senate, a governing body on which three to six hundred members of the most prominent families served. They made policy, which was then enforced by magistrates from their own ranks, with two annually elected consuls as the highest public officials. All citizens could cast their votes in two popular assemblies: the *comitia tributa* and the *comitia centuriata*. The democratic character of the two assemblies differed significantly. In the first, voting was done by district. The vote of every citizen, rich or poor, counted equally. It was here that the lower magistrates were elected: the aediles (responsible for public works) and the quaestors (supervisors of the state's finances). However this assembly was not entirely independent, since people's voting habits were regularly influenced by patronage ties to the

1

elite and senatorial intimidation. In the *comitia centuriata* the population was divided into five classes based on wealth. The wealthier citizens were in the first class and furnished the majority of votes. In such a system the election of praetors (responsible for the administration of justice and authorised to lead armies) and consuls (entrusted with general civil and military authority) was a matter for well-to-do citizens. The poor inhabitants of Rome, who formed the overwhelming majority, played no role in this assembly.

During the Republic, the Romans steadily expanded their power. In the fifth and fourth centuries they had their hands full conquering Italy, a process that was completed around 270 BC. They then turned their attention to the Mediterranean world and conquered the countries bordering the Mediterranean Sea one by one. The Carthaginians and the potentates of the Greek-Hellenistic world in the east soon realised that the Romans could not be stopped. At the end of the first century BC, the Mediterranean Sea could justifiably be called *mare nostrum* ('our sea'). The Romans, however, were not satisfied with that and went to war with the Germanic tribes in central and western Europe as well. They too were made to learn that in the long run the Roman legions were invincible.

These great conquests led to a change in mentality among the elite. As a result senatorial solidarity, which had made Rome great, gave way to individualism. Increasingly consuls who had achieved stunning military successes began to act on the basis of self-interest, keen as they were on acquiring great personal power. The repercussions of this are not hard to guess. Internal rivalries began to emerge, leading to a power struggle that was fought out during the first century BC. Sulla and Marius, Pompey and Caesar, Antony and Octavian: these are the leading players in the civil wars of the dying Republic. After Caesar had paved the way for sole sovereignty as 'dictator for life', it was ultimately Octavian who dealt the Republic its death blow, by solemnly declaring himself *princeps*, first citizen of the state, in 27 BC. His reign was the beginning of the Principate, generally referred to as the Imperial Period.

In the history of the world there have been few rulers who had greater power and ruled over a vaster area than the Roman emperors. In the first two centuries of the Common Era they reigned from Britain in the west to the Euphrates in the east and from the Sahara in the south to the Rhine and the Danube in the north. They levied taxes and made life and death decisions. Most emperors had a solid power base: they were enormously wealthy, ensured of the support of the armies and constantly surrounded by large groups of flatterers who could read their every wish. Influential people who dared to plot against them or contradict them were putting their lives at risk. The people no longer played any significant role. The popular assemblies no longer met, and the only way the crowds could make their voice heard was by cheering for or booing the emperor during the circuses or gladiatorial matches.

Powerful though the emperors were, there was always a degree of uncertainty about how far they could go. Whenever they made decisions with negative consequences for the Senate, they could expect serious protests. After all, they nominally still ruled in consultation with that ancient advisory body. The emperors had to respect that partnership, even though everyone knew that an accumulation of functions meant that they had almost unlimited power. But to dispense with the Senate openly, thereby blatantly flouting tradition, was dangerous. It was not unheard of for senators to let the emperor know that his authority, though great, was not unlimited and that his formal powers were not officially set down anywhere. Emperors who went too far in the eyes of the senators were criticised. Most of the time the criticism would die down after a while, but occasionally the emperor got the message that he had better watch his step.

Things only really became dangerous for an emperor when not only the Senate but also the imperial guard (his personal bodyguards), the army and the people of Rome expressed their discontent. When that happened his fate was sealed. But this did not mean a return to calm. Instead of closing ranks and making a concerted effort to find a new emperor, all parties involved put forward their own pretenders to the throne. A civil war was the result, and stability was a distant memory. It was some time before an emperor was firmly in the saddle again.

The worse the situation in the Empire, the more vulnerable the position of its most powerful man. In the first two centuries of the Imperial Period, most emperors were in power for many years and passed away peacefully, apart from a few emperors who had relied too much on their own counsel. Only in 69, after the death of Nero, did the situation become critical. Three emperors in a row met with violent ends. In the third century the Roman Empire was a mere shadow of what it had been during the first two centuries. The co-operation between the Senate and the emperor had been replaced by anarchy and individualism. Emperors no longer came from the Senate by definition; soldiers from the provinces who had worked their way up through the ranks to become generals were now assuming control of the highest office. They were able to stay in power as long as they enjoyed the backing of the military, but it became increasingly difficult to meet the growing demands of the armies stationed along the Empire's borders. Emperors and rival emperors succeeded each other at a rapid pace. Every emperor was under near constant threat of assassination, even before he had been well and truly installed on the throne. There was, however, no shortage of pretenders to the throne. New candidates were constantly stepping forward in the hope that they would be able to do what their predecessors could not, namely, survive on the throne. This was something almost no one in the third century succeeded in doing. Of the twenty-one official emperors and numerous rival candidates who believed they were in command during the troubled period 235–284, only one died a natural death. The remainder met a sorry end. They were killed by enemy soldiers or died at the murderous hands of men in their own circles, or in their despair saw no other way out but to take their own lives.

At the end of the third century and the beginning of the fourth, Diocletian and Constantine managed to put a stop to the decline, but the Empire never again attained the stability of the first two centuries and the emperors could never be sure of their lives. The final decline began in the second half of the fourth century. Financial deficits resulting from decreasing production and mounting internal tensions accelerated the reversal. Maybe those factors themselves would have led to the downfall of the Empire, but the unforeseen threat of barbarian attacks, to which the authorities had no response, accelerated the process of decay. This process progressed more rapidly in some regions than in others, with the decline of the west being more dramatic than that of the east. The emperors paid for this with their lives.

After the division of the Roman Empire by Theodosius in 395 the differences between the east and the west were plain for all to see. The west was disintegrating, and in 476 the central Roman authority was replaced by Germanic principalities. In the east the emperors had a well-stocked treasury at their disposal, which made it possible to buy off possible attacks by the Huns or Germans and recruit mercenaries on a large scale. Thus Constantinople and the surrounding lands could be defended from attack, and the Eastern Roman Empire continued to exist as the Byzantine Empire until 1453, when the Turks under Mehmet the Conqueror captured the capital of Constantinople (Byzantium).

4

This book is about the last days of all the Roman emperors, a subject about which we are reasonably well informed thanks to ancient historians. Even the last days of emperors who were in power for just a few weeks did not escape the writers' attention. We read how some emperors faced death valiantly, resigned to the transience of life, and showed their best side during their final moments. But there were also those who were unable to cope with their approaching end. However disastrous their reigns had been, they refused to believe that their death was the direct consequence. Eye to eye with their murderers they could do nothing but beg for mercy, hide or crawl into the arms of a dominant mother.

Although the Roman Empire officially begins with Octavian Augustus in 27 BC, I begin my story with the murder of Julius Caesar in 44 BC. As a dictator for life he laid the foundations for the imperial system. I conclude in 476 with Romulus Augustulus, the west-Roman emperor who was deposed by the German army officer Odoacer. In the east emperors remained in power after 476, but I have not included them here because from then on one could no longer speak of a Roman Empire with Rome and Italy as its centre.

I felt I should mention a few important facts about each emperor's private and public life in order to allow certain connections to emerge between life and death. My account of the emperors' deaths is based mainly on primary sources, with the secondary literature playing a supporting role. I have elected not to give literal translations of the relevant texts, choosing instead to tell the story in my own words. The most important reason for this is that most emperors' deaths were described by a number of authors but, more often than not, these accounts differ substantially from one another. I thus was able to select the most plausible version, while at the same time incorporating details from other authors. For the reader who wants to peruse the accounts of emperors' deaths in the source material, I have included the most important texts for each emperor at the end of each entry.

I have tried to deal with the emperors in the correct order. For the first two centuries this was not hard, as one reigned after another. The death of an emperor cleared the way for his successor. From the third century onwards it becomes problematic because there were years in which several emperors were in power at the same time. Since this book is primarily about the end of emperors' lives, I have decided to base the order on the dates of the emperors' deaths. Whenever an emperor lived on anonymously as a private citizen for a number of years after being deposed, I chose the year in

which he was forced to abdicate as 'the end'. I make an exception for
Diocletian, who voluntarily stepped down in 305 but whose name
continued to circulate regularly in political circles until his death
in 311 or 312.

In the interest of readability I decided not to give an emperor's
complete name, confining myself to the name under which he has
become known. Thus I do not talk about Nero Claudius Caesar
Augustus Germanicus or about Marcus Opellius Macrinus, but
simply about Nero and Macrinus. Only in cases when an emperor
has gone down in history under a double name do I use both names.
Marcus Aurelius and Septimius Severus are good examples of
this. For the exact dates of the reigns and the death dates I have
relied on D. Kienast's *Römische Kaisertabelle: Grundzüge einer römischen
Kaiserchronologie.*

Sources

The available source material is very uneven. There is a whole story
to tell about the deaths of some first-century emperors. For a number
of emperors of late antiquity, on the other hand, it is difficult to put
together an adequate account of their deaths because the information we have is often nothing more than a one-line statement that
an emperor has died or was killed. Fortunately the deaths of most
emperors were discussed by several authors, and thus by combining
a number of superficial statements we can get a more detailed picture
of their final days.

For the emperors of the first century we can fall back on a few
authors who have written extensively about their activities. In the
first place we have Suetonius (*c.* 70–*c.* 125). This scholarly recluse
was the author of an extensive oeuvre, with his best-known works
being his imperial biographies, which describe the lives of the
first twelve emperors, from Caesar the dictator to Domitian. In a
short, succinct style, bereft of frills, he tells of their lives, their appearance, their qualities, their politics and their relationships – in short
all the things that made a biography compelling reading according
to the standards of the day. Suetonius uses a set method in his biographies, dividing his work into sections of related topics, which are
then treated in some depth. There is no shortage of juicy details in
his narrative, and he is not shy about including gossip and scandal.
He pays special attention to an emperor's final days and succeeds in
creating an atmosphere in which an emperor's death is discussed in
the context of the life he has led.

For a few emperors from the first century we can also make use of the writings of Tacitus. This historian – according to many the greatest of classical antiquity – lived from about 56 to 117, sketching a dark picture of the Roman Empire in his *Annals* and *Histories*. He makes no secret of his dislike for the imperial system. He proceeds with great care, basing his work on senatorial archives, memoirs and eyewitness accounts. Unfortunately some of what he wrote has not come down to us, and so there is not enough material to do a full-scale comparison of his version of events with that of Suetonius. But the surviving descriptions of emperors' deaths betray a deep psychological insight.

Finally, for the first century there is also Cassius Dio (*c.* 160–230). This Greek author wrote an eighty-volume history of Rome, from the founding of the city to 229, during the reign of Severus Alexander. He trots out a lot of facts, but his treatment of the material is insufficiently critical. Events that *might* have happened a certain way are described as if they actually *did* occur that way. There are large gaps in his historical narrative – only the books covering the years 69 BC to AD 46 have come down to us intact – but these lacunae are partially filled by the summaries that others have made of his work.

Cassius Dio's account is also the most important source for the second century, along with the *Historia Augusta*, a fourth-century collection of biographies of emperors and rival emperors from 117 (the death of Trajan and the accession of Hadrian) to 284 (the death of Numerian and the beginning of Diocletian's reign). It is still unclear whether the biographies were written by six different authors or were the work of one man, although in recent years scholars have tended towards the view that a single author was responsible for the entire text. It is highly entertaining reading, but the historical reliability is often questionable.

The last two decades of the second century and the first thirty-eight years of the third century, up to the reign of Gordianus III, are also described by the Syrian Greek Herodian, who lived around the year 200. He is a good source for what was happening in Rome during that period. One moment his style is rather sensationalistic, and the next it is moralising. He devotes much attention to the emperors, and thus their final days as well.

The entire third century is covered by Aurelius Victor (second half of the fourth century). Two of his works on the emperors have survived: the *Liber de Caesaribus* and the *Epitome de Caesaribus*. In the form of a compendium he gives a brief history of the emperors in

both works, starting with Augustus. The last emperor discussed is
Theodosius I, who died in 395. Brief though the biographies are, he
always attempts to treat the deeds of the emperors in terms of their
characters. The striking details give his work a special quality.

A contemporary of Aurelius Victor by the name of Eutropius
wrote a short history from the founding of the city of Rome to the
death of the Emperor Jovian in 364. He is also an important source
for the third (and the fourth) century. His strength lies in his choice
of material and the good characterisation of the central figures.

Two Christian authors offer a special perspective on the events
of the third and the early fourth centuries. The first, Lactantius
(c. 250–c. 314), wrote a book entitled *On the Death of the Persecutors*,
in which the emperors who were guilty of persecuting Christians
are put through the ringer. He takes pleasure in having the persecutors meet the grisliest ends possible. His credibility, however, is
debatable. The second writer is Eusebius of Caesarea (c. 260–340),
bishop and personal friend of Emperor Constantine. He wrote a
history of the church and a biography of Constantine. He is strongly
biased, particularly in the latter work. The whole biography exudes
the atmosphere of a tendentious encomium. In Eusebius' eyes Constantine can do no wrong; his political opponents, predominantly
pagans, are the villains of the piece.

Had it not been for the work of Ammianus Marcellinus (c. 330–
395), much of what took place in the middle of the fourth century
would have escaped our attention. He is the last great pagan writer
in a world that was increasingly dominated by Christians. For that
reason alone it is worth getting acquainted with his ideas. Although
a Greek, he wrote his Roman history in Latin. He begins with the
accession of Nerva in 96 and ends with the defeat of the emperor
Valens in 378 by the Goths in the battle of Adrianopolis. Unfortunately the first thirteen books, which cover the period up to 353,
have been lost, but the eighteen books between then and 378 make
up for a lot and offer a nice counterweight to the Christian authors.
Thanks to Ammianus Marcellinus we are able to form a picture of
Emperor Julian 'the Apostate' (361–363), whom we could have
otherwise judged only on the basis of later, Christian writers, who
were hostile to him.

The fourth century and a large part of the fifth also have a place
in the work of Zosimus, a Greek historian who lived at the end of
the fifth century and the beginning of the sixth. As a pagan he is
regarded as the polar opposite of Lactantius and Eusebius. Emperors
who were excoriated by the Christian authors were praised by

INTRODUCTION

Zosimus. His information is not very exact; he is quick to sidestep complicated issues and lets us know any number of times how much he regrets that the old traditional gods have been replaced by the Christian God. The emperors' deaths are described in a short and concise fashion. One notices that his account differs on more than one occasion from those of other historians. Two texts by a pagan author, who was called Anonymus Valesianus by his seventeenth-century publisher, form a nice supplementary source. The first text sketches the life of Emperor Constantine I, while the second treats the period 474–524.

Aside from that, our knowledge about the fourth and fifth centuries comes mainly from Christian sources. Ambrose of Milan, Augustine of Hippo, Jerome, Arnobius and Orosius are of course the most important Christian writers of the late fourth and fifth centuries, but they were not terribly concerned with the lives and deaths of the emperors and make only indirect reference to the supreme rulers. Since these writers do not offer a coherent history of the emperors, the historical narrative of the fifth century must be pieced together from other, highly diverse sources. First of all there is the *Ecclesiastical Histories* of Socrates Scholasticus, a fifth-century lawyer and church historian. Comparable to this work is the church history of his contemporary Sozomenus. Both of them sometimes have very salient information that is not to be found in other sources. Then there is Philostorgius, who also writes about religious issues, discussing the role of the emperors in that context.

The chronicles of John of Antioch, the historical work of Gregory of Tours and the writings of Procopius of Caesarea from the sixth century also examine the history of the Empire from the sidelines. The authors are frequently ill-informed, as can be seen in their accounts, which are not coherent narratives but a series of disconnected statements. Far more informative is the chronicle of the world up to 1118 by Zonaras, a twelfth-century Byzantine monk. He has drawn from various authors and appropriated the information he felt was most relevant. Finally there are a few authors who are little known or have remained anonymous but who from time to time suddenly make a well-chosen observation. Their texts were compiled by Theodor Mommsen in *Chronica Minora*, Volumes I–II, Berlin 1892.

I consider myself fortunate to have had the help of a good friend while working on this book. Vincent Hunink read through the text with a critical eye. His marginal comments saved me from a number of jarring slips. I would also like to thank Susan Breeuwsma of Athenaeum–Polak & Van Gennep publishers for a pleasant working relationship.

A long series of dreary deaths could depress a modern reader. Personally I had no problem with this while writing. Even more pleasant was the fact that my wife Marianne was always willing to listen to the sorry end of yet another 'disturbed' emperor, even late at night, which is usually when I would bother her. With concern in her voice she would often ask me, 'Those emperors aren't driving you crazy, are they?' I can now answer her question once and for all in the negative. In full possession of my mental faculties I dedicate this book to her.

Oegstgeest, June 2001

1

THE JULIO-CLAUDIAN
EMPERORS

CAESAR
13 July 100 BC–15 March 44 BC

Gaius Julius Caesar, scion of an old patrician family which could trace its origins back to Aeneas, the Trojan forefather of the Romans, was unquestionably a special man. This is a point all historians can agree on. In his public as well as his private life he was a bundle of contradictions. Sometimes he was merciful like no other, while at other times he displayed immense cruelty. He preached moral virtue but regularly flouted the rules of decorum. In the power struggle among the elite in the later years of the Roman Republic, he took risks his political opponents were afraid to take, and that was what made him so dangerous to them.

He had a brilliant career, starting from his first appearance on the political stage. Even at a young age he was the darling of the common people of Rome. In 60 BC, together with Pompey and Crassus, he formed a triumvirate, a private agreement to govern the state. The collapse of the Republic was in fact already apparent. In 59 BC Caesar arranged it so that he would be elected consul and could go to Gaul after his term in office. There he waged a merciless war, returning to Rome in 51 BC a rich and powerful man. It did not surprise anyone when he demanded more than the consulship. The republican system did not offer the necessary scope for his ambitions. He got even with his rivals, vanquishing the last of them, Pompey, in 48 BC. After that his power was practically unlimited. In 46 BC he became dictator for a period of ten years. Because he was also *pontifex maximus*, high priest of the Roman state religion, and had loyal legions at his disposal, he believed he was secure in his position. But he had not reckoned with the frustrated senators. After his victory over Pompey he assumed that his position was universally recognised and consequently did not bother to eliminate his political opponents. That attitude gained him a large republican opposition. However, he was not afraid, certainly not in February 44 BC, when he became a dictator for life.

Fear was not part of Caesar's character. This was already apparent in his younger years when a ship bound for Rhodes on which he was travelling was captured by Cilician pirates. They put a ransom of twenty talents on his head, an enormous sum, but Caesar insolently informed them that he was worth at least fifty. The pirates had a good laugh and let a few of Caesar's companions go in order to get the ransom. In the meanwhile Caesar treated the pirates as if they were his personal bodyguards, ordering them around and leaving no doubt as to who was in charge. They played along and went on laughing even when he told them that after his release he would come back to take revenge. As soon as the ransom was paid Caesar was set ashore. He went to Milete, put together a fleet and went back and did exactly what he said he was going to do. Every pirate he was able to catch was crucified. Because they had treated him well during his captivity, he had their throats slit before they were put up on the cross, as a token of mercy.

Caesar had defied danger his whole life, but for that very reason, in 44 BC he was not sufficiently aware that he was far more vulnerable than his exalted position might have caused one to suppose. A number of senators were bent on revenge. They wanted the Republic back, and there was no place for Caesar there.

The Ides of March, 15 March: a date that can be found in any history textbook. It is the day Caesar was assassinated. The conspiracy against him had been well prepared. Approximately sixty people were involved, among them senators, ex-consuls and ex-praetors. The ringleaders were Brutus and Cassius. Although the conspirators kept their plans secret, the plot seems to have been leaked, and Caesar was warned that his life was in jeopardy. But he disregarded all advice and paid no heed to prophecies about his impending demise. He took no notice of the words of the soothsayer Spurinna that he should be on his guard for a threat that would come to pass no later than the Ides of March. On the eve of the murder he dined with 'friends'. A discussion ensued about what was the most preferable way to die. Caesar was the only one there to make a case for a quick, unexpected death. That night he dreamed he was floating above the clouds and shook Jupiter's hand, but the meaning of all this did not sink in. He only began to have his doubts when his wife Calpurnia told of a dream she had had in which the façade of their house collapsed and her husband was stabbed to death in her arms. He briefly considered staying at home, but Brutus asked him not to disappoint the waiting senators and persuaded him to come.

The attack was well planned; it was set to take place three days before Caesar was to leave for the east to fight the Parthians. The Senate would convene in the Curia of Pompey. Caesar had himself carried in on a sedan chair. When he stepped out, Artemidorus of Cnidus, a Greek scholar who apparently knew of the conspiracy, came up to him with a scroll in his hand. He handed Caesar the scroll. When Artemidorus saw him pass the scroll to a servant he told Caesar to read the text as it contained important information for him. But Caesar did not listen and walked on. At the entrance to the Curia stood the soothsayer Spurinna. Caesar saw him and said, 'The Ides of March are here and nothing has happened.' Spurinna replied, 'Indeed, the Ides are here, but the day is not over yet.'

Caesar entered the Senate and the senators rose to greet him. He walked through their midst to his seat, just in front of the statue of Pompey. A number of senators positioned themselves behind his chair, and a few of them walked up to him as if they had something to ask him. Tillius Cimber was the first to address him. When Caesar refused him and told him he would have to wait, Cimber grabbed Caesar's toga at the shoulders with both hands. Caesar tried to break free and cried out, 'This is violence!' At that moment the other conspirators leapt into action. One of the Casca brothers stabbed Caesar in the back of the neck, but he reacted instantly, grabbing Casca's arm and stabbing him with his stylus. Caesar tried to get away, but the thrust of another dagger made escape impossible. He now saw the raised daggers pointing at him on all sides.

Caesar had been a proud man all his life, and he remained so in his final struggle. He realised he could no longer escape his fate, but he did not want anyone to see him die in his own blood. He covered his head with his toga and simultaneously pulled down the folds of his garment over his feet. The senators stabbed him twenty-three times with knives and daggers, but he endured it all without saying a word, uttering only a quiet moan when he felt the first knife go in. When Marcus Brutus fell upon him, he is said to have asked, 'You too Brutus?' The physician Antistius later said that of all the wounds, only one had been fatal.

The conspirators intended to throw Caesar's body in the Tiber, but fear of Caesar's political ally Mark Antony, who was then consul, made them change their minds. Caesar's body was carried back to his house by three devoted slaves. After the reading of the will at Mark Antony's house, the magistrates and ex-magistrates carried the dictator's body to the Forum on an ivory bed of state. There was some hesitation about whether the funeral bier should be burned in the Temple of Jupiter Capitolinus or the Curia of Pompey. Just then two people suddenly set the bed of state alight with candles. Bystanders threw everything they had with them on to the fire, even jewellery. Later a marble pillar was erected on the Forum, and inscribed on the pedestal were the words, 'For the father of the country.'

Cassius Dio 44.17–19
Suetonius, <i>Caesar</i> 80–89
Plutarch, <i>Caesar</i> 63–66

AUGUSTUS
23 September 63 BC–19 August AD 14
Emperor from 16 January 27 BC

Octavian Augustus is without a doubt the most important figure in Roman history, since it was he who put an end to the Republic once and for all and gave form to the power monopoly that was the Roman Principate. He is also an enigmatic figure with often inscrutable ideas, who has been criticised and glorified, reviled and admired. Whatever we think of him, we cannot ignore the fact that he brought peace and order to the Roman world. A prominent power-seeker in the last days of the Republic, he would become the peacemaker *par excellence*.

The senators who thought they would be able to restore the Republic after Caesar's assassination were disappointed. The veterans of Caesar's wars, the people of Rome and the residents of the other Italic cities wanted nothing to do with their plans and waited for the moment when one of Caesar's political allies would appeal to them. The first contender was Mark Antony, who was supported by Lepidus, the second in command during Caesar's dictatorship. The power strategy Antony had devised was rudely disrupted by the interference of Octavian – then still called Octavius – who had been adopted by Caesar in his will. Neither Antony nor the Senate took the eighteen-year-old Octavian seriously, but he soon made it clear that he was not to be trifled with. The Senate was forced to grant him a wide range of powers, but their hesitancy in offering him the consulship led to a reconciliation between Octavian and Antony, which took shape in late November 43 BC in the famous triumvirate of Octavian, Antony and Lepidus. They were given the powers of consuls, the right to issue edicts and appoint magistrates and the authority to execute citizens without the right of appeal to the popular assemblies. Then they did what Caesar had not done: they massacred the senators who were not able to take flight in time.

Many senators sought refuge in the Balkans, where Caesar's murderers Brutus and Cassius were gathering troops from all parts of the east. Even so they had no chance against the forces of the triumvirate. On 23 October 42 BC the Republican Army met with a crushing defeat. Back in Italy the triumvirs divided the territory amongst themselves. Antony received the eastern provinces and the part of Gaul that lay north of the Alps, Octavian the western provinces, Lepidus was fobbed off with control of Africa and from then on played only a minor role.

The rivalry between Antony and Octavian began to intensify. In the spring of 39 BC their differences in opinion could only be resolved with great effort. As a sign of their renewed co-operation Antony married Octavian's sister Octavia. But that marriage could not prevent the rivals from drifting apart. Antony began acting more and more like a Hellenistic monarch and did so with the encouragement of the Egyptian queen Cleopatra, whom he married in 36 BC. After that he became increasingly estranged from Roman traditions.

In 32 BC the alliance between Octavian and Antony came to an end. From the east, Antony called for Octavian to be driven out and the Republic to be restored. Octavian's propaganda was more effective. He appealed to the people of Rome and Italy to undertake a punitive expedition against the impending menace from the east. On 2 September 31 BC, in the naval battle of Actium on the west coast of Greece, victory belonged to Octavian. Antony's efforts to keep Octavian out of Egypt were in vain. His troops deserted and

Antony committed suicide. Cleopatra did the same when Octavian failed to respond to her advances. Two years later Octavian returned to Rome. He was now the *de facto* sovereign, the commander of a gigantic army and an enormous fleet, but his position of power had yet to be legitimised in any way.

Octavian wanted to be more than a military despot who had reached his dominant position by violence and who, with the backing of the army, could nip any future opposition in the bud. He wanted to give his reign a constitutional basis. Everything he did was intended to convince the Senate and people that he was an acceptable leader for all Romans. With that thought in mind he convened a solemn session of the Senate and the popular assemblies in 27 BC. He was well aware of the fact that too much power would alienate the Senate and the people and would greatly decrease the chance for a peaceful regime that could count on the consent of the populace. Violence would constantly rear its head, and he would have to respond to it with ever-greater violence. The arrangements he made are a reflection of these thoughts. Admittedly his authority was greater than anyone else's, but the powers that were offered to him were within the rules of the old Roman Republic. He was named consul and at the same time received the *imperium* over a few provinces where peace and stability were precarious. In this way he could present himself as a legally elected magistrate who respected the rules of the Roman Republic. He did, however, accept the title *Augustus*, 'the exalted one', the one who stood above parties, a designation that had hitherto been reserved only for gods. He was addressed as *princeps civitatis*, first citizen of the state. The term would become a designation for the form of government that now commenced: the Principate. In the years that followed, Augustus steadily expanded his position of power, assuming, among other things, the authority of tribune, which in the traditions of the Roman Republic made him the protector of the interests of ordinary Romans.

Augustus' constitution was such that over the course of time it has been described in a wide variety of ways, ranging from a transition to a militarily backed monarchy to a complete restoration of the Republic. The ancient writers are likewise split in their views about Augustus' performance. The poets Virgil and Horace, who were members of Augustus' circle, both wrote positively about his performance in office, because he saved the state from the horrors of a civil war and as *princeps* did everything to bring about peace. A century later Tacitus was less enthusiastic and wrote candidly in his *Annals* that Augustus had enticed the soldiers with gifts, the people of the city with grain and everyone with the pleasures of peace. In his opinion the old Republic was further away than ever, because senatorial freedom, which so typified the Republic in its glory days, was now definitely a thing of the past. Augustus himself was always firmly convinced that he had promoted citizens' involvement in the fortunes of the state by incorporating traditional Roman values into his new form of government.

During his rule Augustus paid a great deal of attention to the issue of security within the Empire. In the last century of the Republic the armies were composed of recruited farmers and volunteers. In no sense was there any permanent reserve of troops. Augustus changed this system, abolishing the practice of calling up soldiers in times of emergency, and began building up standing armies. From 15 BC the army numbered twenty-eight legions of six thousand men. The main task of the legions was to guard the imperial borders, which were fortified and interlinked, forming a line of defence, the *limes*. His attempts to move the Rhine border northward to the Elbe ended in failure. In AD 9 three legions led by Varus ventured over the Rhine border into the Teutoburger Wald, but they were routed by the Germans under Arminius. This defeat put an end to the Roman expansion in the north. From then on Augustus pursued a policy of consolidation.

Augustus wanted to make the new age visible in all sorts of ways, especially in the capital Rome. The city itself underwent a veritable metamorphosis. Augustus' words are well known, quoted by Suetonius: 'I found a city of brick and left a city of marble.' This pronouncement must be seen in light of his ambition to make Rome into a place that could compete with the Hellenistic cities of the east. The Temple of Apollo on the Palatine, the Porticus Octavia on the Field of Mars, the Curia Julia and the Basilica Julia, his Mausoleum, the Theatre of Marcellus and his imperial Forum are the visible proof of that ambition. This project of urban beautification was more than just a matter of aesthetics. For Augustus the city's new look was a means of making visible the political, moral and religious changes. One of the cornerstones of Augustus' construction campaign was *pietas*, respect for the gods, one of the old traditional Roman virtues. Augustus' *pietas* was expressed most dramatically in the temple on the Forum Augustum, dedicated to Mars Ultor, the most authentic of the Roman deities, patron of agriculture, father of the city founders Romulus and Remus and the avenger of the death of Augustus' stepfather Caesar. In the niches along the semicircles and colonnades on either side of the Forum stood 108 statues, on the one side the great heroes of Rome's past, on the other side the great men of the Julian line, starting with Aeneas, the forefather of the Romans. The two rows met in the centre at the great statue of Augustus, as a sign of the link between the new age of Augustus and the old Republic.

There were those in Rome who were already contemplating worshipping Augustus as a god during his lifetime. Nothing like that had ever happened before. It is hard to say if Augustus would have refused such a tribute during his lifetime, since in 29 BC, two years before he officially became princeps, during the dedication of a temple to *divus Julius* (the deified Julius Caesar), he seized the opportunity to do some self-promotion and had himself designated as *divi filius* (son of a god) on coins.

In the eastern half of the Roman Empire the cult of Augustus arose fairly spontaneously, since the inhabitants were already accustomed to worshipping the rulers of the Hellenistic states as divinities. Without detracting from the popularity of the traditional gods, the cult of Augustus spread rapidly across the east. Augustus was not worshipped as one of the traditional gods, to whom individual citizens could turn to beg to be cured of a disease. Augustus was presented by the priests of the cult as the man who personally brought about peace, calm and prosperity through his many good deeds. Such cults achieved two aims. In the first place they propagated the ideology of a mighty Roman ruler who cared about the needs of his subjects, and in the second place the fervour with which the cult of Augustus was practised could serve as an indication of the urban populations' loyalty to the emperor. In the west the worship of Augustus never reached the same size and spontaneity.

Augustus reigned for forty years, an unprecedented length of time, which contributed to the stability of the system he devised. At the end of his reign there were only a few people left who had actually been alive during the Republic. Nevertheless Augustus was well aware of the fact that there were senators who longingly looked forward to the time when the Republic, which they had begun to idealise, would be restored. Because he suffered a number of serious illnesses during his years in office, he began taking precautions early on to guarantee the continuity of the system. Even so, his search for a suitable successor was doomed to failure. Since he had no sons himself, neither with his first wife Scribonia, nor with Livia, with whom he shared the rest of his life, he initially had in mind the sons of his daughter Julia and Marcus Agrippa, his most devoted friend. In the end he adopted Tiberius, the son of his second wife Livia, though he had had his misgivings about him in the past. In order to prevent a power vacuum from opening up after his death, during his lifetime he gave his future successor great powers, which did not differ significantly from his own. In this way he was able to secure the system.

Augustus' death was like his reign, calm and peaceful. In the summer of AD 14 he was an old man of nearly seventy-seven who felt his strength diminishing and realised death would not be much longer in coming. The first sign to presage his approaching end was the flight of an eagle. During a sacrificial ceremony on the Field of Mars the bird in question circled Augustus a few times and then flew off to a temple, landing on the first letter of the name of his dead friend Marcus Agrippa. That letter M was interpreted as the first letter of *mors* ('death'). Not long after that, the first letter of his name Caesar Augustus melted after being struck by lightning. The explanation for the destruction of the letter C was that he had only a hundred (Latin: *centum*) days to live. After that time he would join the ranks of the gods, since the Etruscan word *aesar* literally meant 'god'.

Death found him not in Rome but in Nola, in Campania. In spite of his frail health he had set off on a trip to Beneventum with his intended successor Tiberius. They reached Astura where, on board a ship, Augustus was overcome by severe attacks of diarrhoea, presumably the result of a serious intestinal illness that he had been suffering from for some time. Nevertheless he sailed on and spent four days in his villa on the island of Capri. He then crossed over to Naples, where, sick as he was, he attended the games in his own honour. He resumed his journey to Beneventum, but on the way home his illness rapidly worsened.

In Nola he was near exhaustion. He gathered his friends round his sickbed and spoke with them about his succession and the future of the Empire. Finally, with a great sense of drama, he asked them if he had done well in his role in the comedy called 'Life'. Suetonius then has him say, 'If it has pleased you, then clap for the play and dismiss us with applause.'

He remained conscious for a very long time. It was not until he cried out in a moment of fear and doubt that he was being carried off by forty young men, that those present realised that the end was near. After that he sent most of his friends away and remained there with a few intimates. He kissed his wife Livia and suddenly passed away. His last words are said to have been, 'Livia, live mindful of our marriage. Farewell.'

Although almost everyone was convinced that he had died a natural death, stories nevertheless began circulating that he had been poisoned by Livia to clear the way for her son Tiberius. She is alleged to have smeared poison over some figs Augustus was going to pick in his own garden. To divert any suspicion she ate a few figs herself that she had not poisoned. Shortly afterwards he set off on a journey, and it was at that time that the sickness began to reveal itself. It is hard to say if there is any truth to this story, but given Livia's reputation as a ruthless woman, her involvement should not be ruled out.

Augustus' body was brought from Nola to Rome, where the senators outdid one another in paying tribute to the late emperor. After two eulogies, the first by his successor Tiberius, the second by Tiberius' son Drusus, the body was carried to the Field of Mars and burned. An ex-praetor later claimed that he had seen Augustus' soul rising up to heaven. His ashes were gathered up by a number of prominent knights and interred in the Mausoleum. On 17 September, three days after the funeral, Augustus was deified by the Senate.

Suetonius, *Augustus* 98–101
Cassius Dio 56.29–42

TIBERIUS
16 November 42 BC–16 March AD 37
Emperor from 17 September AD 14

Tiberius was already nearly fifty-six when he succeeded Augustus. Few would ever have predicted that he would become emperor. Up to that point he had had an ordinary, unspectacular career and only came to Augustus' attention late in life. At Augustus' insistence he divorced his wife Vipsania and married Julia, Agrippa's widow and Augustus' daughter. He was given a few military commands, including supreme command over the troops in Pannonia and Germania. In 6 BC his relationship with Augustus became strained. He divorced Julia and retreated to the island of Rhodes. There was little prospect that he would ever get back in Augustus' good books. But the death of his intended successors Lucius Caesar and Gaius Caesar forced Augustus to make overtures to Tiberius. In AD 2 Tiberius returned to Rome, and two years later, on 26 June AD 4, he was adopted by Augustus. He was now seen by all as Augustus' successor and was gradually given more powers. In 13 he became *de facto* co-emperor.

After Augustus' death Tiberius was able to present documents to the Senate that officially named him as Augustus' legal successor, thereby guaranteeing the continuity of the monarchy. However, the contrast with the easily approachable and tactful Augustus was great. The sources portray Tiberius as a rather mysterious and complex figure, intelligent and shrewd, but at the same time subject to depressions and attacks of melancholy, which would leave their mark on his reign.

He knew perfectly well that he was not especially popular. None the less his relations with the Senate were reasonably good. He transferred the power to elect magistrates from the people's assemblies to the Senate, but this measure did not lead to an improvement of his relations with the latter body. In his paranoia he had many senators put on trial for *lèse-majesté*, which could encompass a wide range of charges. These trials were an efficient method for the emperor to sentence difficult or recalcitrant senators to death. Some senators escaped condemnation by taking their own lives.

As chief administrator of the Empire Tiberius functioned well during the early years of his reign. He followed the pattern set by Augustus and maintained strict control over the governors of the senatorial provinces. The military successes in Gaul, Germania and Armenia during his tenure in office were principally the work of his nephew Germanicus. Many believed that Tiberius, jealous of the popular Germanicus, had had a hand in the latter's death in the year 19.

Over the course of his reign Tiberius grew more introverted. In 26 he left Rome and retreated to the island of Capri. A confidant of his, the commandant of the imperial guard, Sejanus, did the honours in Rome, but his wayward conduct cost him his head in October 31. The last years of Tiberius' life were full of bitterness. Illnesses and a fear of betrayal made him even more paranoid than he already was. The countless trials for *lèse-majesté* alienated the Senate from him completely. His only contact with Rome was by correspondence, and this was mainly in order to have people he suspected of being ill-disposed to him put on trial. If we believe Suetonius, Tiberius' days on Capri were filled with sexual perversions. He had never made any real arrangements for his succession. There were only vague indications that he had designated Gaius, the son of his late nephew Germanicus, as his successor.

On 16 March 37 Tiberius' life came to an end. He died, seventy-eight years old, in a villa in Misenum. An unknown sickness, which was accompanied by stabbing pains in the side and a high fever, had revealed itself a short time before, when he had decided to make one last visit to Rome. He had left Capri and the best part of his trip was behind him, but twelve kilometres from Rome a bizarre incident caused him to change his plans: a tame snake he often played with was devoured by a swarm of ants. He saw this as a warning to beware of the wrath of the masses. He turned around and went back to Campania.

There are many stories about the exact circumstances his death. In all probability he died of natural causes in Misenum, exhausted by illness and fever. According to the orator Seneca (the father of the philosopher-politician Seneca), when he felt the end was near he took off his ring and held it in his hand for a time, as if he wanted to give it to someone. Then he put it back on his finger. With a balled fist he lay there motionless in bed for some time, alone, with no servants nearby. He is said to have called for them, but without result. He tried to stand up, but his strength failed him and he collapsed next to his bed.

It is also possible that Tacitus is right. He tells of a famous doctor, Charicles, who was regularly consulted by the emperor even though he was not his personal physician. Tiberius also sought the doctor's advice during the last weeks of his life. After a visit Charicles gave the emperor his hand, ostensibly out of courtesy, but in reality to do a quick check of his pulse. Tiberius noticed it, and it unnerved him. As if he wanted to show that there was nothing wrong with him, he had a dinner prepared for himself and stayed at the table longer than usual. Nevertheless Charicles assured Macro, the prefect of the imperial guard, that the life was slowly draining out of Tiberius and it would be a matter of days before he gave up the ghost. After that, everything was set into motion to prepare the provincial governors for the imminent farewell. On 16 March Tiberius' breath grew laboured and it was thought that death was near. Gaius entered the villa, thinking the moment had come for him to assume the reigns of power. He was already being congratulated, but the jubilant mood turned sour when word came that Tiberius had opened his eyes and had asked for something to eat. General confusion, no one knew what to do. Only Macro kept a cool head. He went into Tiberius' room and gave the order to throw the covers over him, thus suffocating the emperor.

A third version of events openly speaks of murder, claiming that he had been poisoned by Gaius, who had set his sights on the throne and thought things were taking far too long. In this scenario Tiberius was the victim of a slow-acting, undetectable poison.

When the news of his death reached Rome, the people took to the streets, crying out, 'Throw him into the Tiber' and 'May Mother Earth and the gods of the underworld give him a place among the damned.' In spite of the people's hatred the soldiers brought his body to Rome. In a solemn ceremony he was interred in the Mausoleum of Augustus. He was not deified.

Tacitus, *Annals* 6.50
Suetonius, *Tiberius* 73; *Caligula* 12
Cassius Dio 58.28

GAIUS
More commonly known as Caligula
31 August 12–24 January 41
Emperor from 18 March 37

Gaius seemed to have all the makings of a popular emperor. He succeeded an unpopular emperor, and he was the son of Germanicus, who had attained a mythical status since his death under suspicious circumstances. He had spent much of his youth in his father's army camps, where the soldiers gave him the nickname Caligula ('little boots'), because he would tramp around in soldiers' boots (*caligae*) that were too big for him. His childhood was not a happy one. After the death of his father he was immersed in a world of murder, suspicion and paranoia. He first lived with his great-grandmother Livia, then with his grandmother Antonia, and from 31 to 37 he lived on Capri with Tiberius.

He had only just accepted the imperial title when things started to go awry. There is no way of knowing if this was because of his troubled upbringing, his fearsome appearance, which elicited repugnance and revulsion among many, or the fact that he suffered from epilepsy. The only thing we do know for sure is that almost everything he did ended in disaster. As an administrator and military commander Caligula left a great deal to be desired. Most of the campaigns he undertook are ridiculed in the sources. His military operations in the north were a particular source of amusement. Diversions in the forests beyond the Rhine, during which Caligula combed the woods, stripped the trees of their branches and then gave them the form of trophies by hanging weapons on them, were not exactly conducive to a good image. Even more ludicrous was his expedition to the coast of the English Channel. He directed his forces to take up battle positions on the beach, without the soldiers knowing what he was planning to have them do. All of a sudden he ordered them to gather shells, which he dubbed 'the spoils of the ocean, destined for the Capitol and the Palatine', and fill their helmets and pockets with them.

His reign was a concatenation of cruelties. Countless people were executed, sometimes following the most ghastly humiliations. It made no difference if they were from the senatorial class or the urban proletariat; everyone was a potential target. He sank to new depths of depravity after being told that it was getting too expensive to buy sheep to feed to the wild animals and decided on the spot that prisoners who had been sentenced to death should be thrown to the animals. In his madness he even went so far as to have a temple built to honour him as a god. Inside the temple there was a statue that was dressed in whatever Caligula happened to be wearing that day. Flamingos, guinea fowl and pheasants were sacrificed daily in the temple. He is also said to have wanted to appoint a horse as consul.

His extravagances were legion. He had magnificent villas and country estates built; he bathed in warm and cold perfumes, sailed on ships with pearl-encrusted sterns, organised costly games and spent days tossing coins off the roof of the Basilica Julia to the crowds gathered below. To finance all this he levied enormous taxes.

He had quite a tempestuous sex life. He would sleep with actors and prisoners from the provinces, but he nevertheless preferred women. Whores or women he picked up off the street, his own sisters or wives of universally esteemed senators, it made no difference to him. For Caligula, where there was a will, there was always a way. He would regularly invite prominent Romans with attractive wives out to dinner. When the women lay down at the foot of his couch, he would look them over like a slave trader inspecting his slaves, lifting up their heads with his hand if they looked down in embarrassment. Then he would leave the dining hall and call over the woman who had pleased him the most. He would return a short time later and launch into a detailed description of the woman's body and sexual abilities.

There was no shortage of plots to assassinate him, but there was no one who dared to risk mounting an attack on his own.

In January 41 things had got the point where a few people seriously began putting their heads together to plot an assassination. Remarkably, the initiative did not come from a senator but from Cassius Chaerea and Cornelius Sabinus, both of whom were officers of the imperial guard. Chaerea loathed Caligula because of the humiliations to which the emperor continually subjected him. Although Chaerea had a martial appearance, Caligula constantly made fun of him for having a high-pitched voice. Every day when he came to ask the emperor for the password of the day, he was greeted with 'Venus' or 'Priapus' (the garden-god with the erect phallus). Time and again he was mocked as a weakling and a sissy, often in the presence of others. For a long time he ignored Caligula's insults, but at a certain point he could bear them no longer and set out to kill the emperor. Chaerea's fanatical commitment to killing Caligula had a contagious effect on others, even a number of senators, particularly the ex-consul Valerius Asiaticus, whose wife had been seduced by the emperor, an accomplishment Caligula had described in detail during a banquet. Quite a few senators and knights joined Chaerea, some for opportunistic motives, others because they hoped to restore the Republic.

Caligula knew nothing of Chaerea's plans, though a short time before an oracle had told him to beware of 'Cassius', but he took that to mean Gaius Cassius, the governor of Asia and a descendant of the Cassius who was behind Caesar's assassination. He did not have an inkling that the warning referred to Cassius Chaerea.

The conspirators decided to kill Caligula on the last day of the games that were being organised in memory of Emperor Augustus. They planned to strike at the end of the day's programme, in a narrow corridor. The time was well chosen; thousands of people would be there, making it extremely difficult for the emperor's bodyguards to spot the conspirators in the crowd. As the highest-ranking soldier Chaerea would be able to get close to the emperor in order to ask for the password of the day, and therefore it was decided that he should be the one to strike the first blow.

The authors Cassius Dio, Suetonius and Flavius Josephus, all of whom wrote about the assassination, differ on what exactly happened next, though it is not hard to get a rough idea about the course of events. Caligula was having a grand time of it. He threw fruit at the spectators and watched in amusement as they fought over it. The conspirators grew restless as Caligula showed no sign of leaving the theatre. Finally he stood up and left by the exit that led to the palace complex. There he wanted to bathe and look at young boys whom he had had brought over from Asia to sing hymns that had been specially composed for him.

When Chaerea, armed with his sword, sidled up to the emperor, he was given the password 'Jupiter', to which Chaerea replied, 'So be it', thereby invoking Jupiter as god of vengeance. He did not hesitate for a second and immediately took a swing. Caligula's jaw was split, but the blow was not fatal. Was it a last twinge of fear of the much-hated emperor that made him miss at the decisive moment? Those who knew him later said that Chaerea had deliberately not wounded Caligula mortally. He wanted Caligula to die a slow death. Caligula was able to flee, but he did not get far; he was caught by Sabinus, who grabbed hold of him and tripped him. The other plotters rushed forward and stabbed him like savages, carrying on even after he was dead. Some of them even sank their teeth into his flesh. The honour of administering the *coup de grâce* was given to Aquila, but everyone knew that in reality Chaerea deserved sole credit for having killed Caligula.

Caligula's German bodyguards came to his aid, but to no avail. However, they did kill a few conspirators who were not able to get away in time. Caligula's body was secretly brought to a villa of the Lamia family. It was partially cremated on a hastily built funeral pyre and buried under a layer of sods. At first no one wanted to believe that Caligula was dead. There were those who suspected that he had fabricated the news of his death himself to see how people would react. But in time everybody realised the truth. Caligula's statues and portraits were destroyed. His memory had to be completely eradicated. His wife and daughter were also killed.

Flavius Josephus, *Jewish Antiquities* 19.1–273
Suetonius, *Caligula* 58–59
Cassius Dio 59.29

CLAUDIUS
1 August 10 BC–13 October 54
Emperor from 24 January 41

The hope that many senators cherished of restoring the Republic was quickly dashed by the soldiers of the imperial guard. They regarded a return to the Republic as not in their best interest and therefore undesirable. Because they realised that the Senate would also recognise that a restoration of the Republic was unrealistic and would thus agree to appoint a new emperor, they decided to take the initiative themselves. They chose the person who, in view of their loyalty to the Julio-Claudian dynasty, was most suitable: Claudius, Caligula's uncle. On the day of the murder he had sat next to Caligula for some time but had left the theatre shortly before the attack. After Caligula's death became known, he fled to a remote corner of the palace and hid behind a curtain. He was discovered there by a soldier of the guard. He thought that his number was up, but the soldiers proclaimed him emperor and brought him back to their camp.

The Senate was presented with a *fait accompli* and agreed that Claudius be formally invested with the powers of *princeps*. He had hardly any experience in government and had always been regarded as a somewhat unworldly scholar who stumbled over his words and had difficulty walking. His leadership skills were ignored by Emperor Tiberius; he was not made consul until 37, during the reign of Caligula. The lack of any long-term experience in public office did not, however, prevent him from developing into a good emperor.

Claudius understood that a good relationship with the Senate was essential and treated this institution with respect. But whenever he suspected his life was in danger, he showed no mercy. During his reign no fewer than thirty-five senators and more than three hundred knights were killed. Among that number were men who had tried to oust Claudius, but there were also those who had done no wrong. They fell victim to the accusations of Claudius' third and fourth wives, Messalina and Agrippina. Senators were also falsely accused by freedmen who enjoyed the emperor's implicit trust.

In 47 Claudius found the Senate openly opposed to him when, in his capacity as censor, he proposed allowing prominent Gauls into the Senate. He pressed ahead with his plans anyway, just as he also implemented his resolution to grant civil rights to the provinces on a large scale. Despite his lack of experience, Claudius was no disgrace as a soldier. His principal accomplishment was the annexation of south-east England, which was established as a province.

He made the people of Rome beholden to him by placing the distribution of grain under his personal supervision. To safeguard the grain transport he had the harbour of Ostia built. Henceforth the large cargo ships from Alexandria could go there and would no longer have to call at Puteoli and transfer their loads to smaller ships. He also offered the people recreation in the form of gladiatorial matches. It is hard to say who enjoyed them more: the urban proletariat, who had a day out, or the emperor, whose fondness for cruel and bloodthirsty spectacle was well known.

Claudius was unhappy in his married life; he had a total of four wives. He was no match for the machinations of his last two wives, Messalina and Agrippina. With the former he had a daughter, Octavia, and a son, Britannicus. From the sources a picture emerges of Messalina as a nymphomaniac and devotee of orgies. In 48, when Claudius was in Ostia, she went so far as to marry Gaius Silius, who had just been elected consul for the following year. Both of them were executed. Claudius swore he would never get married again, but that same year he succumbed to the charms of Agrippina, who brought along her son, Domitius. For Claudius this was the beginning of the end.

Claudius' entire life was dominated by his fear of being murdered. Extra security measures and severe punishments had nipped every attempted assassination in the bud. However, he was powerless against Agrippina's scheming. She was appropriating ever more power and had even been given the official title Augusta, which had previously only been granted to Augustus' wife Livia. She received foreign delegations and wore a military cloak that was decorated with gold embroidery. But she wanted more; she wanted her son Domitius to be emperor. The first step in that direction was taken in 50.

Domitius, who was three years older than Claudius' biological son Britannicus, was adopted by Claudius on 25 February 50 and given the name Nero. Britannicus gradually faded from the scene, and Nero became the intended successor.

Claudius died on 13 October 54. Although there are a few scholars who, given the conflicting accounts in the sources, believe he died a natural death, it seems certain that he was the victim of foul play. The instigator was Agrippina, who felt the time was ripe for her son Nero to take power. She was annoyed by a remark Claudius had made to the effect that it was his lot in life first to put up with his wives' misdeeds and then to have to punish them. According to Tacitus she decided to poison Claudius, but it took her some time to make up her mind about what type of poison to use. It must not work too fast, that would rouse suspicion; but it should not take too long either, because then there was a danger that Claudius would realise something was amiss and appoint his son Britannicus as his successor after all. She, or one of her underlings, sought contact with Locusta, a notorious dealer in poisons. The poison was given to Claudius by Halotus, a eunuch who usually tasted Claudius' food before serving it to him. But according to Suetonius we should not rule out the possibility that Agrippina administered the poison herself. He claims she soaked mushrooms, a favourite food of Claudius', in poison and served them to him. This later caused Nero to remark that mushrooms were a divine food, because thanks to eating them Claudius became a god.

It is not reported how long Claudius remained alive after that. It was rumoured that he immediately lost the ability to speak and died the next morning, following a night of unbearable pain. But there are other possibilities. Perhaps the poison worked well, but not as well as was hoped, because, as often happened, Claudius had got drunk during the meal and vomited it all up, or had had diarrhoea. Agrippina was thrown into a state of panic. She appealed to a physician, Xenophon, who masqueraded as a helpful doctor. According to this scenario it was he who actually poisoned Claudius once and for all, by feeding him a bowl of poisoned gruel or by injecting a fast-acting poison into his throat.

Claudius' death was kept secret until all arrangements had been made for Nero's succession. The official story was that he was ill and the gods were being implored to spare his life. When it came time for the news to be made public, Agrippina conspicuously sought solace with Claudius' son Britannicus, embracing him and saying how much he looked like his father. But she made sure that he did not leave the room until after Nero had presented himself as the new emperor. Around noon Nero left the palace, accompanied by Burrus, the prefect of the imperial guard. At a sign from the prefect he was greeted with cheers by the soldiers and lifted into a sedan chair. That same evening, in a carefully orchestrated session of the Senate, he was presented with the insignia that went with the imperial rank.

One of Nero's first decisions was to order Claudius' deification. He was buried with all pomp and circumstance in the Mausoleum of Augustus.

Tacitus, *Annals* 12.64–67
Suetonius, *Claudius* 43–44
Cassius Dio 60.34

NERO
15 December 37–9 June 68
Emperor from 13 October 54

Nero has gone down in history as one of the worst emperors. Some think he was even more depraved than Caligula. His administration was steeped in treachery and murder. Everyone, high or low, family or stranger, lived in fear of his bloodthirsty nature.

Initially there was no reason to suspect things would turn out that way. Right after his accession Nero acquired the support of the praetorian guard and also gained senatorial backing with a speech in which he held out the prospect of restoring the original Augustan constitution. He had outstanding advisers in the philosopher Seneca and the soldier Burrus, who kept him in line for the first five years. But after Burrus' death in 62, Seneca faded into the background and Nero revealed his true nature.

Within the family circle the first victim had been claimed in 55. It was Nero's stepbrother Britannicus, who was poisoned. His mother Agrippina, no angel herself, was the next victim, in March 59. His two wives, Octavia and Poppaea Sabina, were also unable to escape his cruelty. It is said that Nero personally kicked the pregnant Poppaea to death when she criticised him for coming home late from the chariot races. He was obsessed with violence. It was whispered that he would comb the streets and public houses at night with friends in order to find people to beat up. He was also no stranger to sexual violence. He was a menace to men as well as women. His most notorious affair was with a man, Sporus, whom he loved passionately. Nero had him castrated and treated him as his wife.

The most notable event of Nero's reign was the fire of Rome. In July 64 an enormous conflagration reduced a large part of Rome to ashes. To this day historians still debate whether Nero, who was in Antium at the time the fire broke out, was involved in the disaster in some way. Rumours suggested he had had a hand in it because he wanted to rebuild Rome into a more beautiful city and create space for his dream project: the construction of the *domus aurea*, a royal palace of unparalleled beauty. Nero himself blamed the Christians, at the time still a small minority in Rome.

It should come as no surprise that in the last year of his reign Nero was vulnerable to conspiracies. In 65 a coup under the leadership of Piso ended in failure. The perpetrators, including the poet Lucan, were put to death or forced to take their own lives. Three years later there was success. Nero had just returned from a tour of Greece, where, as he said himself, his artistic qualities were given the recognition they deserved, when in March 68 the news reached him that Julius Vindex, governor of Gallia Lugdunensis, had risen up in rebellion. He had the support of Galba, the governor of Hispania Tarraconensis. This did not do Vindex much good, and in May he was defeated by the Rhine Legions. The soldiers wanted to proclaim their commander Verginius Rufus emperor, but he declined the offer. If Nero thought that he was now in the clear, he was mistaken. Galba's henchmen in Rome managed to win over many a senator to their cause. It was only a matter of time before Galba would be appointed emperor. The defection of Nymphidius Sabinus, the commander of the imperial guard, was the final blow for Nero.

In his palace on 9 June, Nero sensed that the end was near and that he should not count on clemency. He knew that his enemies would be looking for him and his only option was flight. But where to go? He considered various possibilities: he could go to the Parthians as a supplicant, throw himself humbly at Galba's feet, or, and the sources consider this to be the most likely option, he could go to Egypt, in the hope that he would be made governor there. But that hope quickly vanished when he realised that even the palace guard had deserted him. He sent slaves to call his friends in the guest wings, but they returned empty-handed. Then he walked past the doors to the sleeping chambers himself, but everyone had fled. He went back to his bedroom only to discover that even his personal bodyguards had now left him. They had even taken away the little box of poison he always kept on hand. He toyed with the idea of throwing himself into the Tiber, but decided against it in the end.

One of the few who remained loyal to him was Phaon, a freedman. He offered Nero his villa, which was located between the Via Salaria and the Via Nomentana, approximately six kilometres from the palace. The emperor gratefully accepted the offer. In the company of Epaphroditus, a freedman whom he had been close to, and Sporus, his beloved, he rode there on horseback. It was an ignominious retreat. Dressed only in simple clothes and with his head covered so as not to be recognised, he looked nothing like the flamboyant emperor he once was. A dark omen reminded him that his end was near; not that he needed any reminding, of course. On his way to Phaon's there was a small earthquake. It seemed to him that the earth was splitting open and the spirits of all those he had killed were rising up to take revenge.

When he passed a camp of the imperial guard and heard the soldiers shouting as they cursed him and exalted Galba as their emperor, his heart sank. A little further along he was recognised by a passer-by, who hailed him as emperor. Bereft of any illusions he rode on. The company left the horses at a side road and made their way through the underbrush, bramble bushes and reeds to Phaon's estate. Having reached the wall of the house, Phaon asked Nero to hide temporarily in a sandpit, until he could be brought into the villa unseen. Nero balked at the idea of being buried while he was still alive and waited by a pool of water instead. Finally he was smuggled into the house. He rested for a time on a mattress and drank a glass of lukewarm water. He refused the coarse brown bread that was offered to him.

Presently it became clear to Nero that he was not going to escape his pursuers. He asked his companions to kill him, but they refused. Nero heaved a deep sigh and said, 'Have I neither friend nor foe?'

While Nero debated about whether or not to take his own life, Phaon received a note from a messenger. Nero snatched it out of his hands and read that he would be punished in the manner of their ancestors: he would be tied to a post and whipped to death. He took out two daggers and tested the sharpness of the steel but he kept postponing the final deed with the excuse that his time had not yet come. At the same time he cursed the cowardice that kept him from administering the *coup de grâce*. 'This doesn't become you, Nero, get a hold of yourself', he kept muttering. When he heard the horsemen riding in to the grounds of the villa, he jabbed the dagger into his throat, crying out: 'What an artist the world is losing in me!' The wound was probably not fatal, and in the end it was Epaphroditus who put him out of his misery. He was barely thirty years old and had been emperor for fourteen years.

He was interred in the family tomb of the Domitii, on the hill Pincius, visible from the Field of Mars. A porphyry sarcophagus and a marble altar surrounded by a stone balustrade kept his memory alive. For although he was despised by the Senate, the common people, whom he had regaled with imposing spectacles, had loved him. Years later, in the spring and summer, flowers could still be found decorating his tomb.

Suetonius, *Nero* 45–50
Cassius Dio 63.27–29

2

THE YEAR OF
THE FOUR EMPERORS

GALBA
24 December 3 BC–15 January 69
Emperor from 8 June 68

The day before Nero breathed his last, Galba, who had already proclaimed himself emperor, was confirmed as such by the Senate. He was already an old man in his seventies and had lived through all the emperors of the Julio-Claudian dynasty. No one, except perhaps Galba himself, would ever have thought that he would become ruler of the Empire. He came from a very distinguished Roman family, had been consul and proconsul and had also earned his spurs as a soldier. During the reign of Nero he gained a reputation for being someone who had strong feelings about Old Roman discipline. He believed he was the man to restore the law and order that had fallen by the wayside under Nero.

In September or October 68 he left Spain for Rome, accompanied by Otho, the governor of Lusitania, who had joined forces with him. Things started to fall apart almost from the beginning. His advisers proved to be less trustworthy than he had thought; his attempts to repeal the expenditures authorised by Nero did not contribute to his popularity; and his refusal to approve a pay increase for the soldiers of the Rhine Legions and the imperial guard alienated him from the military.

THE YEAR OF THE FOUR EMPERORS

In early January 69 the end was already in sight. The troops in Germania Superior refused to recognise him as their leader and proclaimed Aulus Vitellius, commander of Germania Inferior, emperor. The elderly Galba, whose two sons had both died at a young age, then adopted Piso, a descendant of an old aristocratic family with no political experience, as his son and successor. This decision incurred the wrath of Otho, who had thought that he himself was the leading candidate. Once a friend, Otho was now Galba's mortal enemy, though the emperor only found this out on the last day of his life.

If Galba believed in omens, he must have known from the moment he set foot on Italian soil that his reign would be of short duration. A bull that was set to be sacrificed broke loose after being struck with the axe, and, in an anguished frenzy, it crashed into Galba's chariot, spraying him with its blood. As he got out, the emperor was nearly struck by one of his bodyguards' spears in the ensuing mêlée. The day he adopted Piso the servants forgot to place the ceremonial chair from which he was to address the soldiers on the dais.

The clearest sign of his impending downfall came on 15 January, the day of his death. While he was making a sacrifice on an altar before the Temple of Apollo on the Palatine, a soothsayer warned him that danger was lurking and his murderers were not far away. Otho, by contrast, who was standing behind Galba, interpreted this warning as a favourable omen. He felt sure of success when a freedman came to bring him the message, 'The architect and his contractors are expecting you.' That was the signal that the soldiers of the imperial guard were ready. He slipped away surreptitiously. At the gilded milestone at the foot of the Temple of Saturn he was met by some twenty soldiers, who brought him in a covered sedan chair to the camp of the Praetorian Guard.

After the sacrificial ceremony Galba went to the palace to confer with his advisers. One of them suggested he stay inside the palace, deploy slaves as a means of defence, barricade the entryways and wait; the conspirators would probably reconsider. But most were in favour of meeting the threat head on. Galba chose the more radical option and, protected only by a linen cuirass, readied himself to be carried to the Forum in a sedan chair to address the people; his intended successor Piso was sent to the camp of the imperial guard. This seemed like the right decision, all the more so as it was being reported that Otho had been killed. A soldier even showed a bloody sword with which he supposedly cut Otho down, eliciting from the disciplinarian Galba the query, 'On whose authority?' But the rumours of Otho's death proved to be false. Otho was alive and well and his army of followers was growing by the hour.

Galba had reached the Forum when Piso arrived with the bad news that Otho's men were on their way to overthrow the emperor. Some advised him to go back to the palace, but Galba pressed on. In the centre of the Forum, near the Basilica Julia, knights of the imperial guard suddenly appeared. The crowd that was accompanying Galba scattered. The standard bearer of the cohort that was acting as his escort tore the medallion with Galba's image off the standard and hurled it to the ground. The emperor sat there in his sedan chair on the Forum, trapped between the Basilica Julia and the Lacus Curtius, a defenceless old man at the mercy of his enemies.

Only a few soldiers remained loyal to him. Under a barrage of arrows from the knights the bearers tried to bring Galba to safety, but in their haste they were unable to keep the chair steady, and the emperor tumbled out on to the ground.

According to the sources he faced death bravely, like a general who was firmly convinced he had only acted in the best interest of Rome. He presented his throat to the assassins and exclaimed, 'Strike, if it is for the good of Rome.' A soldier of the fifteenth legion drove his sword deep into Galba's throat. Then the others went at him, badly mutilating his arms and legs. Some soldiers did not know when to quit, continuing to stab him even after his head had been severed from his body. Piso managed to escape to the Temple of Vesta, one of the most sacred places in Rome, but he was dragged out and killed. He was also decapitated.

Galba's head was brought to Otho's camp, stuck on a pole and paraded among the standards of the cohorts. The mutilated body was left on the Forum, as an object of scorn and derision. A former slave of Galba's, Argius, eventually removed it and had it buried in a simple grave in the garden of one of Galba's villas along the Via Aurelia. The next day the head was also found and reunited with the body. All reminders of the emperor were wiped out.

Suetonius, *Galba* 18–20
Tacitus, *Histories* 1.23–49
Cassius Dio 63.4–6

OTHO
28 April 32–16 April 69
Emperor from 15 January 69

When Otho seized power, expectations in Rome were not high. He had the reputation of being a dissolute and idle man with a powerful appetite for luxury. It certainly did not help his cause that he had been a member of Nero's inner circle and that he had shown, with his coup against Galba, that he did not shrink from using violence to achieve his aims. He did not belong to the Old Roman nobility either, his grandfather having been the first member of the family to become senator and his father the first to hold the rank of consul.

Although Otho was only emperor for three months, from 15 January till his death, during that brief reign he did not display those faults for which he had been despised earlier in life but acted in accordance with the dignity of the office. He tried to keep the imperial guard as well as the Senate on his side, but he only partially succeeded. The Senate had difficulty accepting his violent rise to power, and the soldiers of the guard were constantly making new financial demands that he was unable to meet.

However, the real threat to Otho came from outside Rome, from Vitellius, who had been proclaimed emperor by the Rhine Legions. Otho proposed a system of joint rule and was even willing to marry Vitellius' daughter, but the tide could not be turned. Vitellius sent his army to Rome. For Otho there was no other solution but to face the opposing army. On 14 March he left Rome and made camp in Bedriacum, just north of the Po, some thirty kilometres from Cremona. He had no reason to expect a favourable outcome, as his army was badly outnumbered by that of Vitellius.

On 14 April the decisive confrontation took place, somewhere between Bedriacum and Cremona. Otho's forces were defeated. Otho, who had not taken part in the battle himself, was given the news by an eyewitness. The way to Rome lay open for Vitellius' legions. Although a number of friends tried to persuade Otho to continue the fight with the help of legions from the Danube provinces which had just arrived, he believed there was little else to do but flee or take his own life. It was the actions of an ordinary soldier after the battle that ultimately made him choose the latter. He had just told of the defeat, but Otho's advisers accused him of lying and put it to him that he had run away just to save his own life. To demonstrate

37

that he was speaking the truth and was no coward, he fell on his sword before the eyes of Otho. According to Suetonius, who had heard it from his father, Otho supposedly cried out that he could not subject such good soldiers, who were willing to sacrifice everything for him, to any more dangers. In an emotional speech to his staff and soldiers, he announced his decision to end his life. Having to look on as Romans fought Romans was unbearable. For him it was better to die honourably than to watch Romans slaughtering each other. He did not begrudge Vitellius his victory if the gods had so willed it. Then he urged everyone to seek refuge elsewhere and not give the enemy a reason for further bloodshed by being caught.

Afterwards he retired to his room and wrote farewell letters to a few close friends. He burned all the letters he had received the last few months containing negative information about Vitellius so as to prevent the senders from getting into trouble when the letters were discovered. Finally he said farewell to the members of his personal staff with an embrace and a kiss. He was last seen in public when he had to settle an argument between soldiers who wanted to keep fighting at all costs and others who wanted to retreat. At nightfall he quenched his thirst with ice-cold water. At his request two daggers were then brought to him. After making certain that all his friends had gone, he went to bed and enjoyed a good night's sleep. Towards morning he got up, picked up the dagger and stabbed himself in the chest, just below the left nipple. Upon hearing his groans a few servants stormed into the room. He showed them his fatal wound and expired.

Loyal soldiers carried his body off and buried it. Some of them, overcome by grief for their beloved emperor, stabbed themselves to death on his grave.

Suetonius, *Otho* 9–12
Tacitus, *Histories* 2.46–50
Plutarch, *Otho* 15–18
Cassius Dio 63.11–15

VITELLIUS
7 or 24 September 15–20 December 69
Emperor from 2 January 69

Nothing is as fickle as the popular will. The same people who had prayed so ardently for Otho when he left for the north now cheered Aulus Vitellius as their new ruler. His reputation was even worse than Otho's when he had come to power. In his youth he was one of the favourite catamites of the emperor Tiberius, earning himself the nickname *Spintria* ('sphincter artist'). He had the reputation of being a yes-man and a great hedonist, who had been a familiar face in the palace during the reigns of Caligula, Claudius and Nero. Once he gave a banquet at which two thousand exquisite fish were consumed. The only thing he had going for him was his name. He came from a renowned family, and his father had been a public figure under Claudius, holding the office of consul for three terms. He himself had worked his way up to be consul and governor of Africa and Germania Inferior.

He was certainly no soldier. He stayed behind in Germania when his army did his dirty work in northern Italy. Shortly after receiving the news that his forces had been victorious, he went to Rome. During the journey he reportedly indulged in wild binges of eating and drinking. He stopped off in Lugdunum (Lyon) and presented his six-year-old son Germanicus to the troops as a possible successor. He also paid a visit to the battlefield near Cremona, where to the dismay of many he remarked that the smell of dead enemies was sweet, but the smell of slain citizens was even sweeter.

He entered Rome in the middle of July. He proclaimed himself consul for life. Contrary to expectations he showed himself to be a moderate. There were no reprisals: even Salvius Titianus, who had played a role in his brother Otho's coup, was not punished. But dark clouds soon began to gather over Vitellius when he received word that the armies of the east had put forward a rival candidate: Vespasian, a popular general. He was held in great esteem by the legions in Syria and Egypt and before long received the backing of the Danube Legions. Although Vespasian was locked in a fierce struggle with the Jews in Judea and Galilee and therefore could not himself take charge of things right away, it was clear to everyone that he was the one calling the shots.

It was the Danube Legions that put an end to Vitellius' reign. They invaded Italy, and on 24 October, practically at the same spot outside Cremona where Vitellius' army had been so successful before, there was a decisive battle. Vitellius' men were soundly defeated. For four days the victorious soldiers wreaked havoc in the enemy camp and in the city. Vitellius occupied the Apennine Pass in an attempt to halt the advance, but his troops defected in droves. Vitellius had no choice but to retreat to Rome. On 20 December the enemy army reached the gates of Rome. They fought their way into Rome at three points, the Via Flaminia, the banks of the Tiber and the Via Salaria, and conquered the city. The situation for Vitellius was hopeless.

Vitellius had himself brought from the rear wing of the imperial palace to his wife's home on the Aventine. He intended to hide there and escape under cover of darkness to his brother's house in Terracina. But in the end he did not go through with the plan. According to Tacitus, who described Vitellius' last hours in detail, this was because of his indecisiveness and the fact that in his difficult position he misinterpreted even the most obvious things. But perhaps, realising that rescue was no longer a possibility, he wanted to take leave of his wife. After that he returned to the deserted palace. He walked past the rooms, but found no one left to talk to. The eerie silence and the emptiness of the chambers depressed him so much that he wrapped himself in loose-fitting clothing, tied a belt full of gold pieces around his waist and fled into a gatekeeper's booth. He tied the dog he had brought with him to the door, which he then barricaded with a bed and a mattress.

He was found there by a tribune of a cohort of the winning army. Initially he was not recognised. When his true identity was discovered, he first tried to salvage the situation by saying that he had a message for Vespasian. But his appeal to be kept in protective custody fell on deaf ears. His hands were tied behind his back. His torn clothing gave him a pathetic appearance, but there was no one who shed any tears for him. His final journey elicited only repugnance from the populace, not compassion. Some pelted him with horse dung and mud; others tried to hit him or poked fun at his physical imperfections: a red, bloated face brought on by excessive drinking, a fat belly and a misshapen thigh, which caused him to walk with a slight limp. A German soldier could not bear to watch and wanted to spare Vitellius any further suffering. He drew his sword to strike him down, but missed and hit the tribune's ear. He was immediately executed. With their swords pointed menacingly at Vitellius' chin, the soldiers forced him to keep his head up and watch as his statues were pulled down one by one. But however much he was humiliated, it cannot be denied that he retained some measure of self-respect during those final, painful moments. When a soldier tried to get a laugh out of the crowd with scornful remarks, Vitellius retorted by saying, 'And yet I was your emperor.' The soldiers' only response was to kick, hit and stab him even harder. At the Staircase of Wailing he was slowly tortured to death; his head was chopped off, and he was dragged into the Tiber with a flesh-hook. Tacitus ends his account with the observation that the same rabble that had cheered him so enthusiastically upon his accession now dropped him like a brick.

Tacitus, Histories 3.84–85
Suetonius, Vitellius 15–18
Cassius Dio 64.19–22

3

THE FLAVIAN EMPERORS

VESPASIAN
17 November 9–23 June 79
Emperor from 1 July 69

The victor, Vespasian, had yet to show himself in Rome. For the last two years he had had to devote all his attention to the Jewish rebellion against Roman authority in Palestine. But his reputation had preceded him. Many were anxiously awaiting his arrival. He was a man of action, forthright and pragmatic, more a soldier than a politician. He did not belong to the old Roman aristocracy, but had been born into the *gens Flavia*, a family that belonged to the second class, the knights. He had made a career for himself under Claudius, a career that appeared to have peaked when he was made consul in 51. Yet under Nero his star had risen further, and in 63–64 he was proconsul for the province Africa. He had even travelled to Greece in the company of Nero, when the latter demonstrated his artistic qualities there. In 67 he was given the task of restoring the peace in Judea and Galilee. Initially he had played no part in the power struggle in 69. It was only after Vitellius became emperor that he – along with Mucianus, the governor of Syria – rose up in rebellion. On 1 July 69 the legions of Egypt declared their support for Vespasian, followed two days later by the legions in Judea. In August they were joined by the Danube Legions. Vespasian sent Mucianus to Italy with twenty thousand soldiers, but when they arrived they found that the Danube Legions had already paved the way for Vespasian in Italy. The man himself had gone to Alexandria to attempt to get Italy on his side by blocking all grain transports to Rome. He left his son Titus in charge of the war against the Jews and the siege of Jerusalem.

On 22 December Vespasian was granted all imperial honours and privileges. Yet it would be another ten months before he entered Rome. He moved to a palace in the so-called 'gardens of Sallust' and would live there until his death. The new emperor immediately attended to the matter of his succession and declared in the Senate that either his sons would succeed him or no one would.

He accomplished a great deal in the nine years he spent in Rome. He initiated an extensive construction programme and gave the city a new look. The Flavian Amphitheatre, better known as the Colosseum, and the Temple of Claudius are the high points of his campaign of urban renewal. As such projects were extremely costly, he raised taxes. Taxes were also levied on goods and services, even public urinals. When his son Titus objected to this, he held a coin under his nose and asked him if it stank. When Titus replied in the negative, the emperor said that the coin had come from the urinals. *Pecunia non olet* ('money doesn't stink') would become a catchphrase of his reign.

Although Vespasian's reign is regarded as a peaceful one, at the end of his life he was the target of a conspiracy led by Alienus and Marcellus, according to Cassius Dio. That was remarkable, since both were thought to be close friends of the emperor. The details are murky. Alienus was killed immediately after the plot was discovered, while Marcellus was brought before an imperial court and condemned to death. Before the sentence could be carried out, he slit his throat with a razor.

Not long afterwards Vespasian fell ill. He was almost seventy and had been suffering from gout for some time, though it was not that disease that killed him. During a tour of Campania he began to have slight attacks of fever. He returned to Rome and immediately headed off to Aquae Cutiliae, a bathing resort with natural springs in the land of the Sabines, near the city of Reate, a place where he would often seek rest and relief from the heat. There, however, the attacks of fever became more severe. Complications arose since his intestines had become irritated from all the cold water he had been drinking. Although he must have felt quite ill, he continued to fulfil his imperial duties, receiving delegations at his sickbed. Acquaintances later said they had heard him say that an emperor should die on his feet. There is some doubt about whether he actually did die standing up on 23 June 79, falling into the arms of helpers who were supporting him. Similarly, we have no way of knowing if Vespasian actually uttered the words 'I think I'm becoming a god' when he expired during a violent attack of diarrhoea. It is quite possible that he had said this before, when he came to the realisation that his worldly life was over and he would be deified after his death.

And he was. His remains were cremated and interred in the Mausoleum of Augustus. Later, during the reign of Domitian, they were moved to the Flavian Temple. He was succeeded by his eldest son Titus.

Suetonius, *Vespasian* 23–24
Cassius Dio 66.17

TITUS
30 December 39–13 September 81
Emperor from 24 June 79

Suetonius begins his biography of Titus with the statement: 'Titus was the idol and the darling of all mankind.' It did not look as if things would turn that way at first. After his success in Judea, where he had managed to break the siege of Jerusalem, he returned to Rome in June 71. His father had got him involved in government; the two held the office of consul together seven times, and Titus had the authority of tribune and was addressed as 'Imperator'. But perhaps the most important position he held during his father's reign was commander of the imperial guard. Vespasian knew that previous emperors had had trouble with commanders who had broken their oath of allegiance to the emperor, and therefore he appointed his son to that important post. Titus did exactly what his father wanted, ruthlessly eliminating his fathers' confidants at the slightest hint of disloyalty. Thus he had the ex-consul Aulus Caecina executed because he suspected him of wanting to stage a coup. Such actions made him quite unpopular. His reputation suffered even further from his association with catamites and eunuchs and his great love for Queen Berenice, a descendant of a Jewish royal dynasty. Some even saw him as a second Nero.

But from the moment he succeeded his father as emperor on 24 June 79, he became a new man. In the two years and almost three months that he wielded the sceptre, he proved to be one of the best emperors Rome ever had. His cruelty had melted into kindness, and his extravagance had turned into goodwill. He showed evidence of this shortly after taking office. When the cities of Pompeii and Herculaneum in Campania were wiped off the map by the eruption of Vesuvius, he offered help wherever he could. He did the same in Rome when a major fire destroyed parts of the city.

His death on 13 September 81 came as a great shock to the people of Rome. He was just forty-one. Shortly before, he had attended the games to celebrate the opening of the Colosseum and during the closing ceremony he seemed highly emotional and depressed. The supposed reason for his gloominess was that earlier, during a sacrificial ceremony, the animal that was to be killed had broken loose and escaped. It had also thundered on a sunny day. Titus had interpreted these events as bad omens. Perhaps he believed that he was suffering from a terminal disease and did not have much longer to live.

Right afterwards, in low spirits, he left for Aquae Cutiliae. He had got no further than the first resting place when he was overcome by a violent attack of fever. After he was placed in a sedan chair and carried the rest of the way, he reportedly opened the curtains and stared at the sky, lamenting the fact that his life was being taken at such a young age without his having done anything to be ashamed of. Badly weakened, he reached the family house in Aquae Cutiliae, and shortly thereafter he breathed his last, possibly in the same room as his father Vespasian some two years before.

Everything pointed to a natural death, but the cause of death has never been established. It was rumoured that he had died of pneumonia, which he had caught from bathing in warm and cold water.

The Jews had another explanation for his death. They saw it as the work of an avenging God, exacting retribution for Titus' destruction of the temple in Jerusalem. According to them a mosquito burrowed its way into his head and eventually grew to the size of a pigeon. For seven years Titus was supposedly tormented by unbearable headaches, to which, according to the Jews, he ultimately succumbed. He might have been suffering from a brain tumour.

Shortly before his death Titus supposedly said, 'I have but one regret.' Nobody knew what he meant by this. Some thought it was a reference to a relationship he had had with Domitia, the wife of his brother Domitian, although he himself had always denied it. In no time stories began circulating that he had been killed by Domitian, who felt that he had waited far too long for the throne. The details of the gossip vary. Some said that Titus was poisoned with a substance secreted by certain fish, while others claimed that Domitian had his sick brother, who was still breathing and might have been able to live longer, put in a coffin packed with ice and snow, in which he suffocated.

After his death there was no hint of any bad blood between the two brothers. Domitian gave the eulogy and put up a number of monuments in Titus' honour. The nation grieved as if it had lost a family member.

Suetonius, *Titus* 9–11
Cassius Dio 66.26

DOMITIAN
24 October 51–18 September 96
Emperor from 14 September 81

Domitian was a very different ruler from his brother; he was a man with two faces. As a leader he showed his good face, and his record

holds up well against that of many other emperors. He realised that a well-organised system of tax collection was necessary to finance the large expenditures in Rome and the provinces. He made every effort and spared no expense to beautify Rome with great monuments. The Temple of Jupiter on the Capitol and his palace on the Palatine are the high points of an ambitious and spectacular construction programme. In spite of the large expenditures he left behind a well-stocked treasury upon his death. However, there was a marked lack of military success during his reign. He waged a number of border wars, including one protracted conflict with the Dacians, but he was unable to force a breakthrough.

His other face was that of a bloodthirsty, megalomaniacal despot, who cared for no one but himself. At the start of his reign there were no indications that he would get such a negative press. To be sure, he was an arrogant man and repeatedly boasted that his father and brother owed their emperorships to him, but at that time he still seemed like a committed leader who shunned violence. However, in the course of time he began to surround himself with all manner of people, including boxers, fools and dwarves, and his style of government became increasingly autocratic. His relationship with the Senate deteriorated, reaching its lowest point when he designated himself in official documents as *dominus et deus* ('lord and god'). Gold and silver statues of him were put up on the Capitol, and his victories in the quadriga were depicted on triumphal arches. The repressive measures Domitian enacted assumed ever more violent forms. Senators were killed on the basis of unfounded accusations. The only choice left to them was the manner of their execution. Though there were plots to do away with Domitian, they were put down brutally, as in 87 and 89. Senators and knights who were suspected of being involved in the attempted coups were banished or killed, though this did not break the opposition to Domitian. It did make potential conspirators more cautious, though. It was not until 96 that they achieved their goal of assassinating Domitian.

In September 96, according to the sources, Domitian sensed his life was in danger. There were several omens that pointed in that direction. For example there was the dream he had had in which the goddess Minerva, whom he worshipped passionately, had left the room in the palace he had reserved specially for her and could no longer protect it because Jupiter had taken away her weapons. But he was alarmed even more by a pronouncement by the famed astrologer Ascletario, who had predicted his downfall. When Domitian asked if Ascletario could also predict his own end, the astrologer said he would die soon and added that his body would be ripped apart by dogs. The emperor then had Ascletario killed and gave the order that his body be burned on the spot in order to negate the prophecy. But the fire had just been lit and Ascletario's body was not yet consumed when a powerful gust of wind suddenly put out the blaze. A pack of dogs rushed towards the pyre, pounced upon the half-burnt body and began tearing it to shreds, thus fulfilling Ascletario's prophecy. Domitian was now certain that his end was near.

The immediate reason for getting rid of Domitian in September 96 was the execution of two courtiers, his cousin Flavius Clemens and Epaphroditus, the old freedman who had stood by Nero in his final hours and had subsequently been a trusted aid to Vespasian, Titus and Domitian. The deaths of these two men made the conspirators realise that time was of the essence. Quite a few people were involved in the plot, with the highest ranking being the prefects of the imperial guard Norbanus and Petronius Secundus. It is not entirely clear whether or not Domitia, the emperor's wife, knew of the plot. There were six people responsible for executing the plan: Parthenius, Stephanus, Maximus, Clodianus, Satur and an unknown gladiator.

The day before his murder Domitian acted extremely nervously. When he was offered peaches he reportedly said, 'If I may be spared to eat them.' An infected wart on his forehead that began to bleed elicited the reaction, 'Let's hope that this is all.' The next day around noon he wanted to go to his bedchamber to rest a bit, but Parthenius, his valet, made him change his mind, with the announcement that there was someone with something very important to tell him that could not wait. A short time later Stephanus came in and said he wanted to inform the emperor of an impending conspiracy. Domitian let him in and Stephanus sat down opposite the emperor. His left hand was wrapped in a thick woollen bandage, according to Stephanus because he had been seriously wounded, but in reality in order to conceal a dagger. Stephanus handed the emperor a document with the names of the conspirators. While the latter read the text, Stephanus suddenly thrust the dagger into his abdomen.

Now Domitian may have been an odd and paranoid man, but he was also tall and strong. In spite of his injury he put up a fierce defence. With the help of a loyal slave he attempted to grab hold of another dagger that he kept under his pillow, but to his dismay he saw that the blade had been removed. He grabbed Stephanus and tried to wrest the dagger from his hands. In the process he cut up his own hands, but that did not prevent him from trying to gouge out Stephanus' eyes with his bloodied fingers. Locked in mortal struggle they rolled around on the ground. Upon hearing the noise, the other conspirators stormed into the room and fell upon Domitian. He was stabbed seven times, and thus he came to learn that he was not a god.

Domitian's body was placed in a coffin and carried out of the palace on the quiet. His old nurse had it cremated at her villa on the Via Latina and then secretly interred in the Temple of the Flavian Emperors. The Senate was exceedingly glad to hear of Domitian's death and named a new emperor from their own ranks: Nerva.

Suetonius, *Domitian* 15–17
Cassius Dio 67.15–17

4

THE ANTONINE EMPERORS

NERVA
8 November 35–27 January 98
Emperor from 18 September 96

Nerva was past sixty when he was put forward by the Senate. He had held all magisterial offices and was universally respected. The only blot on his reputation was the story that he had abused Domitian as a boy, an anecdote recounted by Suetonius. His reign was too short for us to come to a well-considered verdict on his actions. He did his best to win the loyalty of the Senate and the people. He made a solemn pledge that he would never execute a senator, and he gave the people land and food. In Rome he launched an ambitious construction programme, with a particular emphasis on the aqueducts, which were so important for Rome's water supply. He was less popular with the army. The soldiers mourned the death of Domitian and wanted little to do with the old senator who did not seem to have much interest in them.

The situation became critical for Nerva in the summer of 97, when the commander of the imperial guard, Aelianus, called upon the soldiers to revolt. Nerva showed his best side. He was fearless, even giving the soldiers who had locked him in his palace the chance to kill him. He was, however, unable to prevent them from killing two of Domitian's murderers. Perhaps it was this incident that brought him to the realisation that he was too old for the job and made him decide to appoint a co-emperor. In any case, shortly thereafter, in late October 97, from the Capitol he uttered the words, 'May prosperity shine upon the Senate and people of Rome as well as myself. I now adopt Marcus Ulpius Nerva Trajanus.' Nerva had no sons himself, but in the tradition of the Julio-Claudian emperors he was able to look for a successor within his own family. He reviewed all possible family members, paying attention only to their qualities; in the end he chose someone from outside the family who had earned his spurs: Trajan, a capable and level-headed man, who was loyal to the government and popular with the army. It is remarkable that Trajan, who was at that time governor of Germania Superior, did not come to Rome at once to discuss the course of events with his foster father. He still had not come to Rome when Nerva became gravely ill in January 98.

We know no more about Nerva's death than we do about his time in office. The only thing that is certain is that he died on 27 January 98, probably after suffering a stroke in the first week of January. In the days following his stroke he was plagued by panic attacks. In one such attack he started to sweat profusely and then his entire body began to shiver. He started running a high fever and passed away not long afterwards.

The Senate showered him with the highest accolades. He was given a place among the gods, and his ashes were interred in the Mausoleum of Augustus.

Cassius Dio 68.4
Aurelius Victor, *Epitome de Caesaribus* 12

TRAJAN
18 September 53–7 August 117
Emperor from 28 January 98

The accession of Trajan marked the beginning of an eighty-year period in which the Roman Empire enjoyed its greatest prosperity. Four emperors, Trajan, Hadrian, Antoninus Pius and Marcus Aurelius, would ably lead the Empire, each in his own way. It was Trajan who had the most difficult task: once adopted by Nerva, he would have to convince the Senate and people of Rome that the Roman Empire could be led by an emperor without excesses. He did this in a way that won him universal admiration, at least in so far as the limited source material allows us to make such a judgement, as there is far less information about Trajan than about any other emperor of the first and second centuries. But from everything that has been written about him and from what his successors have said about him, we can only conclude that his reign was good for the Empire. Trajan contributed to that image himself, with what has come to be known as Trajan's Column, which depicts his military accomplishments on the Danube.

Trajan was the first Roman emperor who was not born in Italy. He came from a family that had emigrated from Umbria to Italica, a city in south-eastern Spain, not far from Seville. His father had had a brilliant career in the military, and the young Trajan would follow in his footsteps. His political career did not stagnate under Domitian; on the contrary, he made it all the way to consul. This bit of information is not mentioned in the encomium that was given to Trajan by Pliny the Younger in 100 and published a few years later.

Trajan did not visit Rome as emperor until 100, almost three years after being adopted by Nerva. He remained in the north for the first few years of his reign and visited the legions along the Rhine and the Danube. He knew that Domitian had been popular with the troops and wanted to eliminate the possibility of a revolt against his policies in advance. He did not spend much longer than a year in Rome. In 101 he left again, for the Danube. Over the next several years he waged a fierce war against Decebalus, the king of the Dacians, which was eventually decided in Trajan's favour in 106. Dacia became a new province.

For the next six years he stayed in Rome. He worked on improving the city's infrastructure, had an imperial forum and covered markets built in his honour, organised grand gladiatorial matches with some regularity and had a new harbour constructed at Ostia. But unrest in the east called him away from Rome. He left the capital in 114, never to return. He was not able to finish his fight against the Parthians. Like a second Alexander the Great, he got as far as the Persian Gulf, where he supposedly uttered the words, 'I would surely have crossed over to India if I were a younger man.' But the conflict with the Parthians and the revolts of the Jews in Palestine and the diaspora made it impossible for him to carry out this resolution.

In the course of 117 the first signs of Trajan's declining health began to appear. It is hard to say if this was a consequence of a short stay in Arabia. Cassius Dio speaks of the difficult conditions under which the emperor and his army had to operate: it was hot; there was nothing but desert; and there was a water shortage. To make matters worse, it was almost impossible for either the soldiers or their animals to eat normally on account of the hordes of flies covering their food and drink. Shortly afterwards Trajan fell ill. Initially he ignored his poor health and readied himself for an expedition to Mesopotamia. However, he soon came to realise the seriousness of his illness. Instead of pressing on to the east, he headed back to the west, in the direction of Rome.

He personally thought that his illness was the result of a slow-acting poison he had been given, but because Cassius Dio mentions this in passing, without elaborating on it, it does not seem very likely. Moreover his symptoms were not consistent with poisoning. His circulation was poor, which suggests heart problems. On top of that he had a stroke, which left one side of his body paralysed and caused an accumulation of fluid throughout his body. Near Selinus in Cilicia, which would later be renamed Trajanopolis, he died suddenly on 7 August.

Trajan's remains were brought to Rome, cremated and interred in the column that bears his name. He has gone down in history

as a compassionate emperor, although at both the beginning and
the end of his reign he had a number of prominent Romans killed,
ostensibly because they were plotting against him but in reality
because they were influential and wealthy.

Cassius Dio 68.31–33, 69.1–2
Aurelius Victor, *Liber de Caesaribus* 13

HADRIAN
24 January 76–10 July 138
Emperor from 11 August 117

Trajan was dead, but no arrangements had been made for his succession during his lifetime. But just one day after his death, his widow,
Plotina, and Attianus, the commander of the imperial guard,
announced the adoption of Hadrian. Hadrian was a distant cousin
of Trajan's and was also from the Spanish city of Italica. Because
the troops in Syria had solemnly proclaimed Hadrian emperor on
11 August, the Senate was left with no choice but to accept his
appointment.

We are better informed about Hadrian's comings and goings
than we are about those of his predecessor. The *Historia Augusta*, a
series of imperial chronicles from the second and third centuries
beginning with Hadrian, is a welcome addition to the work of
Cassius Dio. Hadrian is portrayed as a man who knew what he
wanted and was not afraid of making decisions that brought him
into conflict with the Senate. But it is extremely difficult to get to
know the real Hadrian. He was simply too complex and played too
many roles.

The start of his reign was not exactly pleasant. Even before he
arrived in Rome, four ex-consuls were murdered for reasons that
have never come to light. Hadrian himself denied any involvement in the murders and blamed the Senate. His relationship with

the Senate would never fully recover. Even so, this never led to any real animosity because Hadrian proved to be a good emperor, though different from his predecessor. He strove for borders that were easy to defend, formed by the Rhine, the Danube and the Euphrates. To this end he strengthened the imperial borders with fortifications. The most well known of these is Hadrian's Wall, a hundred-and-twenty-kilometre long barrier in northern England, intended to keep the Scots and the Picts out of the province of Britain. He undertook few military expeditions. Only the revolt of the Jews under Simon Bar Kochba in 132 required firm action. The revolt was put down three years later and Jerusalem became a Roman city, in which all religious gatherings of the Jews were banned.

Hadrian has been called 'the travelling emperor' because he lived outside Italy for the greater part of his reign. In the years 121–125 and 128–133 he graced almost every province with a visit. The Hellenic world was of particular interest to him. In many cities he translated his admiration into action by erecting monumental Greek buildings, which kept his memory alive after his death.

Many stories circulated about his private life. He was accused of having affairs with married women and sexually abusing boys. One relationship he had with a man is discussed in some detail by the sources because it ended so tragically. In 130 Hadrian journeyed to Egypt, and throughout the trip a handsome Greek youth, Antinous, was at his side. However, Antinous died suddenly, according to the emperor after falling overboard during a boat trip down the Nile; others claimed that he had wanted to dedicate himself to Hadrian forever and had therefore sacrificed himself after an oracle had told him that by doing so he could pass on the remaining years of his life to Hadrian. Hadrian was devastated and had statues of his beloved erected all over the world. He founded a new city, Antinoopolis, at the place where Antinous had died.

In 136 Hadrian, who was by then sixty, became gravely ill. The man who had defied heat and cold, rain and snow, drought and flood during his journeys was now confined to his bed in Rome. His affliction, which he had been suffering from for years, was probably a form of cancer or tuberculosis. Blood regularly streamed out of his nose. The illness grew rapidly worse, and his physical condition deteriorated visibly. Hadrian felt that he did not have long to live and adopted Lucius Commodus. Some claimed that he had chosen him because he was young and good-looking; it was also whispered that Commodus was Hadrian's bastard son. It was a strange decision because Commodus was not in good health and probably had tuberculosis. Servianus, Hadrian's ninety-year-old brother-in-law, and his grandson Fuscus apparently made some condescending remarks about Hadrian's choice and were made to pay for their indiscretion with their lives. Just before Servianus was forced to take his own life he is said to have cried out during a sacrifice to the gods, 'You know very well, gods, that I have done nothing wrong. There is only one thing I ask of you: make Hadrian long for death, but do not let him die.'

Servianus' prayer was heard; Hadrian got sicker and sicker, and in his despair he longed for the end. He wasted away and lost a lot of blood, and his belly became bloated with fluid. Those who knew him said that the emperor appeared confused and talked to himself about his imminent demise. But death refused to come. To add to his troubles his intended successor Lucius Commodus died and he had to look for a new candidate. He found one in the person of Aurelius Antoninus. But even the thought that his succession had been arranged was of little comfort. After his wife Sabina died he began to loathe life. He now lived in a state of permanent despondency and increasingly withdrew from his immediate surroundings. He believed in two omens that pointed to his approaching end. During a sacrificial ceremony in which he commended Antoninus to the attention of the gods, his toga, which he had pulled over his head in accordance with tradition, slipped off. A short time later his signet ring, in which his portrait was engraved, slid off his finger.

Deeply depressed, he ordered a slave to kill him but the latter disregarded the order. He asked others for a dagger or poison, but everyone refused. Finally he called for Mastor, a strong barbarian with whom he would often go hunting. He showed him the spot where he was to strike the fatal blow and marked it with chalk, but Mastor fled in panic. Hadrian lamented that he could have others killed but was powerless to put an end to his own life.

Hadrian met his end in Baiae, on the Gulf of Naples. Summer in Rome was more than he could bear, and he had himself brought to a place where he hoped to find some relief from the heat. After a few days he sensed that death would not be much longer in coming. He summoned Antoninus and discussed matters of state with him. Shortly after that he died, on 10 July 138, probably in Antoninus' arms. Just before his death he is said to have written the following poem, addressed to his soul:

Ah! gentle, fleeting, wav'ring sprite,
Friend and associate of this clay!
To what unknown region borne
Wilt thou now wing thy distant flight?
No more with wonted humour gay,
But pallid, cheerless, and forlorn.
Translation by Lord Byron

The best part of the twenty years and eleven months that he was in power were spent outside Rome. It took some time before he found his final resting place. Through Antoninus' intercession, he was first interred on the grounds of a villa that had once belonged to Cicero. The senators initially would not hear of a state funeral in Rome. They even tried to have all Hadrian's official decisions nullified, but abandoned that idea when Antoninus pointed out to them that such action would also invalidate his own appointment. That was a confrontation that they preferred to avoid. They relented and even agreed to Hadrian's deification. His body was brought to Rome and interred in the Mausoleum that he himself had designed and that is now a part of the Castel Sant'Angelo, not far from the Tiber.

Cassius Dio 69.20–23
Aurelius Victor, *Epitome de Caesarbius* 14
Scriptores Historiae Augustae, *Hadrian* 23–25

ANTONINUS PIUS
19 September 86–7 March 161
Emperor from 10 July 138

Antoninus proved to be a good choice. He had a reputation for being incorruptible and came from a respectable and wealthy family. Both his grandfather and father had been consul. He had lived in Italy almost his entire life, mostly on the family estate in Lorium, just outside Rome. Because his father had died when he was still young, he was prepared for a political career by his two grandfathers. In 120 he had been consul and in 135–136 governor in Asia. That was the only time he lived outside Italy. He had hardly any military experience, but that may well have been the decisive argument for Hadrian to choose him as his successor. After all, he himself had always been a peace-minded monarch and probably hoped that his intended successor would follow that same line. Upon his adoption Antoninus in turn adopted his sixteen-year-old nephew Marcus Verus and Lucius Commodus, the son of the late candidate-emperor Commodus and just seven years old. From then on they would go through life as Marcus Aurelius and Lucius Verus.

The sources speak of Antoninus' reign in glowing terms. The Senate appreciated his style of governance and granted him the title *Pius*, 'the dutiful'. He secured the loyalty of the populace and the soldiers with financial and material donations. The inhabitants of Italy were pleased with the new roads he had built and the construction of houses and public buildings. In contrast to his predecessor he governed the Empire from Rome or from his residence in Lorium. He had the good fortune that there were no major wars to be waged on the borders and that the legions could easily cope with the skirmishes on the borders with Britain, Mauretania, Dacia and Germania. Antoninus personally made sure that the state coffers stayed full. He reigned for almost twenty-three years, to everyone's satisfaction. He might have been the only emperor who was able to maintain his authority without bloodshed.

Antoninus had always cut an imposing figure, but in his old age he began to walk with a stoop. In order to straighten his back he wore a corset made of basswood boards. He also thought he could harden his body by eating dry bread. But his decline was inexorable, and he was aware his life was coming to an end. In 160, a year before his death, he had named the two adopted emperors Marcus and Lucius consuls for the following year.

His final hours were in perfect harmony with his reign. On the evening of 4 March 161 at his residence in Lorium he had enjoyed a sumptuous dinner, gorging himself on alpine cheese. But that night he vomited repeatedly, and the next morning he was running a high fever. He felt himself grow sicker with each passing day. But even in his death throes he was still preoccupied with matters of state; he spoke of nothing else, even in his troubled sleep. On 7 March he felt that death was near. He called the commander of the imperial guard, his most intimate friends and advisers to his bedside and let them know that he entrusted his daughter and the state to Marcus Aurelius. Then he ordered that the golden Fortuna statue that stood in his bedroom be moved to the bedroom of his intended successor as a sign of the transfer of power. Finally he gave the tribune of the imperial guard the password *aequanimitas* ('composure'), rolled over towards the wall and breathed his last.

The senators tried to outdo one another in praising his sense of duty, his goodness and his intelligence and agreed immediately upon his deification. His remains were brought to the Mausoleum of Hadrian and placed next to the bodies of his wife and two sons, who had died young.

Cassius Dio 89.1–4
Aurelius Victor, *Epitome de Caesaribus* 15
Scriptores Historiae Augustae, *Antoninus Pius* 12–13

LUCIUS VERUS
15 December 130–January/February 169
Emperor from 7 March 161

Marcus Aurelius was born in Rome. He came from a very wealthy family from the Spanish province Baetica. His father's sister was married to Antoninus, which gave an informal quality to his dealings with the emperor. Barely eighteen years old, he was given the title Caesar in 139, and a year later he became consul. Antoninus was so fond of him that he gave him his daughter's hand in marriage. Lucius Verus, who was nine years younger, was clearly in the background. But Marcus Aurelius was not the sort of man to seize power and bypass the interests of his foster brother. Upon his accession he insisted that Lucius Verus be named co-emperor, though it was obvious from the outset that the real power lay in the hands of the older Marcus Aurelius. The partnership would last eight years, until Lucius Verus' death in 169.

By then the times of prosperity and peace in the Empire were already over. Shortly after Antoninus' death, the Parthian king Vologaeses had started making incursions into Armenia. Lucius Verus was sent to the east to put a stop to this. He accomplished his mission, but it was whispered that it was actually General Avidius Cassius who did the fighting, while Lucius Verus amused himself with less weighty matters in the town of Daphne, near Antioch in Syria. In 166 Lucius Verus returned to Rome as a conquering hero, where he continued his wanton lifestyle, regularly visiting brothels and public houses. He reportedly had a casino built in the palace, where he played for high stakes until he was so tired he could not keep his eyes open any more. His conduct was an affront to traditional-minded Romans.

The two emperors were not granted a moment's peace, since by 166 the situation on the Danube border had become critical. Great hordes of Marcomanni and Quadi, displaced by migrations of Goths in eastern Europe, had crossed the Danube and made it as far as the Po Valley. In 168 both emperors left for the north. A year later they returned, unable to halt the German advance for good. In northern Italy, Lucius Verus suffered a stroke in his coach. He began vomiting blood. Paralysed and unable to speak, he was taken to Altinum, a town not far from Venice, where he died three days later, in January or February 169. Rumours immediately began to surface that he had been killed by Faustina, the widow of Antoninus Pius, with whom he allegedly had a relationship. There was even talk that he had been poisoned by Marcus Aurelius. Both of these stories were immediately scotched, incidentally. Marcus Aurelius brought the body of his foster brother to Rome and personally orchestrated every aspect of the funeral. His remains were interred in the Mausoleum of Hadrian, next to those of Lucius Verus' real father Lucius Commodus and his foster father Antoninus.

Scriptores Historiae Augustae, *Marcus Antoninus*
Philosophus 14.7–8
Lucius Verus 9.10–11

MARCUS AURELIUS
26 April 121–17 March 180
Emperor from 7 March 161

For the rest of his reign Marcus Aurelius had his hands full trying to deal with all the problems that had arisen around the Empire. In the Danube territories he succeeded in getting the situation under control, annexing two new provinces, Marcomannia (Bohemia) and Sarmatia (Moravia), in the process. But the threat of new clashes remained. The situation in the east was highly complex. The Parthians had not yet been dealt the finishing blow, and even more worrisome was the fact that Avidius Cassius, the governor of Syria, had himself proclaimed emperor in 175. Marcus Aurelius immediately prepared to depart for the east, but before he was well and truly on his way the rebellious governor was murdered by one of his own officers. Marcus Aurelius declined to see the severed head and gave the order for it to be given a proper burial. He forgave the ringleaders. Marcus Aurelius did not return to Rome but resumed his journey. In the company of his son Commodus he visited Asia Minor, Syria and Egypt, and on the way home he stopped off in Greece as well. In 177 he was back in the capital and officially presented the sixteen-year-old Commodus as his co-regent and successor. Because fighting had broken out again on the Danube border, father and son left for the threatened area the following year. In 179 Marcus Aurelius was still fit enough to lead an expedition against the Quadi, but a year later, during an expedition in Pannonia, the symptoms appeared of a serious illness, which soon ravaged him.

Marcus Aurelius is better known to us than any other emperor. We know his views on life and death from his *Meditations*, which he wrote between 170 and 180. He committed his ideals and doubts to paper without reservation. In these writings he comes across as a sensitive and conscientious man, who sincerely strove to be good and regularly questioned the value of his own actions. In reality he lived in two worlds, the world of his own thoughts and the world in which he was expected to be a leader of men who did not understand his ideas about a cosmos governed by divine providence.

Marcus Aurelius had never been in the best of health. As a child he was frequently ill, but by following a sober, almost ascetic way of life he had hardened his body to the point that he could hold his own athletically with his peers. But in the long run his efforts took their toll. In his writings he thanks the gods that his body held out for so long. For the last ten years of his life he was often tired and dizzy and sometimes coughed up blood, symptoms that suggest a form of cancer, tuberculosis or a gastric haemorrhage. In the last stage of his life, when he had difficulty even keeping food down, his physicians increasingly prescribed opiates for him, leading some scholars to think that he became addicted to narcotics. In spite of his physical infirmities Marcus Aurelius never complained. As a stoic he accepted adversity in his private and public life.

The disease that revealed itself in Pannonia was probably the result of one of the old conditions he suffered from, but there were also those who claimed that he had fallen victim to the plague. He was utterly exhausted, but he was untroubled by his approaching demise. His only worry was his son Commodus, who would presently be succeeding him; without sufficient guidance he ran the risk of ending up just like other young rulers who were not equal to the task and went off the rails. He summoned Commodus and gave him his last life lessons. He asked him never to give up the fight against the Germans.

Marcus Aurelius felt his earthly life was now finished and longed intensely for death. He accepted no nourishment for five whole days. On the sixth day he summoned his friends. He spoke light-heartedly about worldly matters. Death, he said to those gathered round his bedside, was a matter of little importance. When his friends could hardly contain their emotions, Marcus Aurelius rebuked them, saying, 'Why are you all crying for me instead of worrying about the plague epidemic which is claiming countless victims?' As he said farewell to his friends he raised himself up from the pillows and spoke to them about his son. He asked them to be fathers to Commodus and to guide him in his reign. That was the only way they could keep his memory alive. After these words he sank back again, utterly exhausted, and said nothing more. He lived for another day and a night. In the early morning on 17 March it was clear that he would die in a matter of hours. His son visited him at his sickbed, but the meeting was brief because his father sent him away, afraid of infecting him. After that he covered his head and expired. He was one month away from his fifty-ninth birthday.

His remains were brought to Rome and interred in the Mausoleum of Hadrian. The Senate approved his deification immediately.

Herodian 1.4
Scriptores Historiae Augustae, *Marcus Antoninus Philosophus* 27–28

COMMODUS
31 August 161–31 December 192
Emperor from 17 March 180

Commodus was eighteen when his father died. It was the first time since Titus and Domitian that the biological son of an emperor ascended the throne. His reign was hardly a blessing for the Empire; rather his time in power is one of the lows points in Roman history. It is hard to imagine a greater contrast than the one between the philosopher-emperor Marcus Aurelius and his son, who in the course of his reign revealed himself to be an insane and megalomaniacal tyrant. As Cassius Dio puts it, the Roman Empire went from a golden age to an age of copper and rust.

Defying his father's last wishes, right after Marcus Aurelius' death Commodus ended the war on the Danube border by pulling out the Roman troops. During his solemn triumphal procession through Rome on 22 October he showed his contempt for Roman values. In the war chariot that brought him to the Temple of Jupiter Capitolinus he had made room for a notorious man, Saoterus by name, whom he kissed passionately throughout the ceremony.

In the years that followed, Commodus' behaviour grew ever more erratic, and conspiracies began forming against him. The first coup came in 182. It was instigated by his sister Lucilla and his nephew Quintianus. The latter was supposed to stab Commodus to death with a dagger, but the assassination attempt failed because Quintianus hesitated at the critical moment and was disarmed by the soldiers of the imperial guard. Lucilla and Quintianus were executed. The commander of the imperial guard Perennis became Commodus' new favourite and *de facto* ruler as well, while the emperor himself indulged in all manner of amusement. But when Perennis threatened to get too powerful, it was all over for him. After that it was Cleander, a former Phrygian slave who had worked his way up to the position of chamberlain, who took charge of the situation. But he too was executed, in 190, when the populace took to the streets in large numbers to protest at the price of grain, for which they held Cleander responsible. There were constantly plans in the works to assassinate Commodus, but since the emperor was always surrounded by flatterers who passed on every scrap of information that came their way to the emperor, he was able to maintain his position for some time.

Meanwhile his egotism knew no bounds. He would dress up as Hercules, clad in a lion's skin, with a heavy club as a weapon, and regularly performed as a charioteer and a gladiator. He was not blessed with any particular talent, certainly not as a charioteer. He badly wanted to perform in public, in the Circus Maximus, but did not dare to, afraid of a fiasco, and so he would only practise in the palace gardens, shielded from the pitying looks of the spectators. As *venator* ('hunter') he was less reticent and would appear in the arena of the Colosseum in the guise of 'Hercules the Hunter'. One day he shot a hundred bears, not from the arena, as was the custom, but from the balustrade. It was not made terribly difficult for him. The arena was divided into four sections by two perpendicular walls, so that the bears, which were divided into four groups, had nowhere to go. On other occasions he would enter the arena to slit the throats of various domestic animals. He is even supposed to have killed a tiger, an elephant and a hippopotamus, but this was after they had first been caught in nets and placed before him as stationary targets.

As a gladiator he must have been far from impressive, though the audience's applause always made him think that he had turned in a top performance. He selected his opponents himself, never renowned fighters, but people from the audience who had no fighting experience and who were equipped with wooden swords. On one occasion he went so far that he must have disgusted everyone. The story comes from Cassius Dio, who claims to have attended the performance in question. Commodus had all the people who had lost their left foot as a result of disease or accidents brought together in the arena. He tied something around their knees that resembled a snake. They were given sponges instead of stones with which to defend themselves. He beat every one of them to death with a staff and acted as if he were Hercules killing giants. For this performance he demanded the princely sum of one million sesterces.

Commodus' death was entirely consistent with his paranoid, violent behaviour. He had thrown all inhibitions to the wind and planned on celebrating New Year's Day 193 as the day of the refounding of Rome as Colonia Commodiana. Furthermore, on that same day he wanted to have the consuls who had been chosen for the following year killed; the following day he would appear in the arena as consul-gladiator. Commodus told his plans to the chamberlain Eclectus, Laetus, the commander of the imperial guard, and Marcia, his favourite mistress. They tried in vain to make him change his mind. Commodus flew into a rage, and when he retired for his siesta he wrote their names on the top of a list of prominent Romans who were slated for execution. In this way he thought he could rid himself of all his critics.

But Commodus was unlucky. In the house where he was living there was a little boy to whom Commodus had given the affectionate nickname Philocommodus. While the emperor was taking a bath, the boy snatched away the tablet and took it to Marcia. She read the names and screamed, 'Is this the thanks I get for all the love I've given you, you drunk?' She immediately called Eclectus, the chamberlain. Together they decided to inform Laetus as well. They realised they would have to act fast; otherwise it would mean their lives. They quickly hatched a plan. Marcia, who usually gave the emperor his first drink during the evening meal, would mix poison in a large chalice and serve it to the emperor. Everything went according to plan. Commodus took the cup, made a toast and downed the contents. Right afterwards he felt nauseated and dizzy and fell asleep. Eclectus and Marcia sent the remaining guests home, something that often happened if the emperor had had too much to drink. They waited until the poison should have reached his stomach and intestines, but he vomited it up. Afraid that he might recover, they sent a strong youth by the name of Narcissus to strangle him. And so it was that Commodus met his inglorious end. He was only thirty-one and had been able to vent his whims and lusts on the people of Rome for almost twelve years.

Clad in cheap pyjamas, Commodus' body was smuggled out of the palace in the middle of the night like a load of laundry and buried in secret. The Senate and people of Rome felt that Commodus deserved the fate of a common criminal and decided that his body should be dragged to the Tiber with a flesh-hook and cast into the water, but on the orders of Consul Pertinax his body was interred in the Mausoleum of Hadrian. Nevertheless his name was removed from all public buildings and struck from all official lists.

Cassius Dio 73.22–23
Herodian 1.16–17
Scriptores Historiae Augustae, *Commodus* 17
Aurelius Victor, *Liber de Caesaribus* 17

5

THE AFRICAN AND SYRIAN EMPERORS

PERTINAX
1 August 126–28 March 193
Emperor from 31 December 192

Commodus' murderers were afraid that a prolonged power vacuum could jeopardize their position, and so that same day Eclectus and Laetus offered the throne to Pertinax, a man of sixty-six. He was consul, following an extremely unusual career. His father was a freedman, who had named his son Pertinax ('perseverer') to underscore the fact that with much perseverance he had gone far in the wool trade. In the beginning it seemed as if the young Pertinax was destined for a career in education, but when he was about thirty-five he changed his plans and joined the army. His star rose quickly. After a few military commands in Syria, Britain and Moesia, he also held a number of posts in the upper echelons of the civil service. In 171 he became legion commander and in 175 consul. After his period as consul he was governor of Moesia, Dacia and Syria and the city prefect of Rome. In 192 he became consul for a second time.

Pertinax seemed genuinely surprised to be offered the emperorship. He was afraid that his enemies had it in for him. To make sure that it was not a trick, he sent a loyal follower to see Commodus' body. When the man assured him that Commodus was dead, he left quietly – it was still night – for the camp of the imperial guard. At first the soldiers panicked, but after some reassuring words from Laetus and Eclectus they calmed down. Pertinax then gave a speech in which he made it seem as if Commodus had died a natural death and held out the prospect of a premium of twelve thousand sesterces to the soldiers, twice the annual income of an average senator. When he finished speaking a few soldiers began to clap and the rest followed, albeit hesitantly. His relationship with the imperial guard would never be close.

Early that morning he was hailed as the new emperor in the Senate as well. However, he did not have time to give his reign a solid foundation, because from the outset there were enough people in both the Senate and the imperial guard who wanted him gone. As a result of Commodus' exorbitant expenditures government coffers were nearly empty, and Pertinax was forced to hold public sales of Commodus' belongings and levy high taxes, an action that stirred up opposition.

There were a total of three attempts on Pertinax's life. The first took place on 3 January 193, just three days after he was confirmed as emperor. The initiative came from the soldiers of the imperial guard. They put forward an old senator, but at the *moment suprême* he took flight and left the city. Two months later Pertinax was in danger once again. While he was in Ostia to inspect grain shipments, the imperial guard again plotted a coup. This time they wanted to make the consul Falco emperor, but this too ended in failure. The Senate declared Falco an enemy of the state, but Pertinax forgave him with the words, 'As long as I am emperor, may no senator be executed, however just that may be.'

Four weeks later came the third coup. Again it was the soldiers of the guard who were behind it. They were angry that a number of their comrades had been killed following the previous coup. It also rankled with them that Pertinax was a stickler for order and discipline, as they had grown accustomed to a life of luxury and licentiousness under Commodus. Three hundred of them marched on the imperial palace. It was 28 March and that morning, according to the sources, Pertinax had twice made a sacrifice with a negative outcome. The first time it turned out that the sacrificial animal had no heart, while the next sacrificial animal had a liver with no point. A few hours later, the soldiers stormed the palace with lances and swords drawn. Seeing that they were outnumbered the emperor's bodyguards retreated in panic and ran outside. The few soldiers who remained at their posts advised Pertinax to flee, but he regarded that as a cowardly act that was beneath his dignity. Undaunted, he confronted the intruders and addressed them. If the writer Herodian is right, Pertinax died as a 'great man'. With the soldiers' swords pointed at him, the emperor supposedly said: 'My death is of no consequence, for I am an old man and have lived long enough.' He reproached them for the unlawfulness of their actions and accused them of acting out of self-interest. But they would not listen. One soldier exhorted them to show no mercy and pointed his lance at Pertinax's chest. The latter prayed to Jupiter, the god of vengeance, pulled the folds of his toga over his head after the example of Julius Caesar and was then repeatedly stabbed with swords and lances. He had been emperor for less than three months.

The soldiers stuck his head on a lance and took it back to the camp with them. On 9 June he was nevertheless given the recognition he deserved. After a state funeral, during which those present pretended to bury Pertinax's body, he was deified.

Cassius Dio 74.9–10
Herodian 2.5
Scriptores Historiae Augustae, *Pertinax* 10–11

DIDIUS JULIANUS
30 January 133–2 June 193
Emperor from 28 March 193

When the death of Pertinax became known, the general reaction was one of confusion and anger. The people of Rome wanted to lynch the guilty parties, and the senators were concerned about the future. They feared that the soldiers of the imperial guard would put forward a tyrant of the calibre of Commodus. But after a few days, life returned to normal. The people resumed their daily routines, and the senators withdrew to their country estates, as far from Rome as possible. The soldiers believed they had everything under control and were not about to let anyone tell them what to do. In their unbridled greed and lack of discipline they went so far as to sell the leadership of the Empire to the highest bidder.

It is almost impossible to imagine, but it really did happen: the auctioning of the emperorship. It is one of the low points of Roman history, an act that must have filled the senators with disgust.

Yet there were two of them who were prepared to meet the wishes of the soldiers: Sulpicianus and Didius Julianus. The first was an ex-consul, who was at the time city prefect as well as Pertinax's father-in-law; the second was a man from Milan who had held many public offices and had even been consul, but because of his luxurious lifestyle he enjoyed little respect from his fellow senators. Sulpicianus entered the camp and tried to persuade the soldiers to recognise him as their new emperor. But he could not count on much support. From outside the camp Julianus began to drive up the price. Both of them shouted at the top of their lungs that they were willing to pay each soldier thousands of sesterces. When Sulpicianus made an offer of twenty thousand sesterces per man, Julianus topped him by five thousand sesterces. The Empire was sold, and Julianus was the new emperor. Accompanied by the soldiers of the guard he walked off to the imperial palace.

The Senate bowed to the pressure and confirmed the appointment, but the people wanted nothing to do with Julianus, who began acting more and more like a drunkard and a reveller and neglecting his official duties. Word of Julianus' bought emperorship quickly spread across the Empire, and just as in 68–69 after the death of Nero, there were plenty of candidates who longed to seize power.

The first of these was Pescennius Niger, the governor of Syria. He was proclaimed emperor by the four legions there and declared Antioch his provisional capital. There is a good chance that if he had left for Rome right away he could have seized power since he had the backing of the urban populace, but he hesitated and remained in Antioch. The second candidate was Clodius Albinus, the governor of Britain, who was in command of three legions and large contingents of auxiliary troops. The third interested party was by far the biggest threat to Julianus: Septimius Severus, the governor of Pannonia, who was assured of the support of the sixteen legions of the Rhine and Danube armies. On 9 April he proclaimed himself emperor in Carnuntum, not far from Vienna, made a pact with Clodius Albinus almost immediately by giving him the title Caesar and left for Rome at the head of a large army.

Julianus was at a loss as to how to handle the situation. He declared Septimius Severus an enemy of the state and put up barricades throughout the city. Rome resembled a besieged fortress in enemy territory. During Septimius Severus' march through Italy, Julianus lost the plot completely and once again showed his lack of principles.

Now that he could not defeat his rival, he invited him to become co-emperor. The Senate initially agreed, but the senators changed their minds when they saw how Julianus, in a state of deep despair, barricaded himself in his palace with fences and thick doors in the hope that by doing so he could survive.

A day later it was all over for Julianus. A short time earlier the Senate had decided to proclaim Septimius Severus the official emperor and condemn Julianus to death. An officer was given the order to carry out the sentence. He found a solitary, frightened man, abandoned by everyone, even his bodyguards. When the executioner drew his sword Julianus burst into tears and cried out, with an utter lack of self-reproach, 'What evil have I done? Whom have I killed?' He apparently even appealed to the new emperor for protection, but to no avail; the officer was unmoved by his pleas. Julianus had been emperor for sixty-six days. His body was given to his wife and daughter, who buried it in the family plot, by the fifth milestone of the Via Labica.

Cassius Dio 74.16–17
Herodian 2.12
Scriptores Historiae Augustae, *Julianus* 7–8

SEPTIMIUS SEVERUS
11 April 145–4 February 211
Emperor from 9 April 193

Septimius Severus was a very different sort of man from Didius Julianus. He was a soldier and made it clear early on that he would not stand for any nonsense. He had come to Rome at a young age from his birthplace Leptis Magna and had been inducted into the Senate by Marcus Aurelius. After that he had held a large number of civil and military positions in all parts of the Empire. At first he was married to a woman from north Africa, but after her death he married Julia Domna, who came from a prominent family in the Syrian city of Emesa. She would not settle for a position in the background and demanded a leading role for herself. Julia Domna bore her husband two sons: Bassianus, better known as Caracalla, and Geta.

On 9 June 193, seven days after Julianus' death, Septimius Severus entered Rome. He dealt mercilessly with the soldiers of the guard, whom he held responsible for the murder of Pertinax. The ringleaders were forced to parade around their camp unarmed before being executed. The remainder were banished from the city. Faithful supporters of the new emperor took their place.

Septimius Severus' position was not unchallenged, however. In the east, Pescennius Niger had not yet renounced his claims to the throne. From Syria he wanted to head west to seize power, but his advance was halted by the armies of Septimius Severus. It took Septimius Severus more than a year to defeat his rival. He succeeded in doing so in early April 194 on the great plain of Issus. Some five hundred years earlier, Alexander the Great had defeated the Persian king Darius here. Pescennius Niger fled in the direction of Antioch, but he was captured and beheaded. The next year Septimius Severus organised a punitive expedition against the Parthians, who had helped Pescennius Niger, and incorporated a large part of Mesopotamia into the Empire.

Now there was only one rival left: Clodius Albinus, the governor of Britain. In late 195 he was declared an enemy of the state. It is not entirely clear why; perhaps it was because he was apparently in league with certain senators who wanted nothing to do with Septimius Severus. Clodius Albinus then proclaimed himself emperor and invaded Gaul. He had some initial success, but in 197 the tide turned. On 19 February of that year the decisive confrontation took place, not far from Lyon. Albinus was defeated. He fled and hid in a house, but he was discovered and committed suicide.

Septimius Severus was a man of discipline throughout his entire reign. He clamped down on the anarchy that had been rife within the military during the time of Commodus. Loyal soldiers could count on his sympathy; opponents knew not to expect clemency. Along with their supporters, they were systematically hunted down and killed. Stories even began circulating that compared the emperor to the dictator Sulla, who had put countless political opponents and their allies to the sword almost three centuries before. He also dealt harshly with Plautianus, who was, like himself, from Leptis Magna.

He had appointed him commander of the imperial guard, but nevertheless he got rid of him when he, his wife and his sons began to get the impression that Plautianus was becoming too powerful. He used the fortunes of his murdered opponents to restructure the armies and erect monumental buildings in Rome and his birthplace to keep the memory of his reign alive.

Septimius Severus was in Britain in 210 when his health began to take a sharp turn for the worse. He had never been very strong since contracting smallpox in Egypt at a relatively young age. He also had gout, as a result of which he sometimes suffered agonising pain in his feet, which made it impossible for him to perform his representative tasks. In 202 when he was to hold a triumphal procession in Rome, he was unable to stand on his own two feet and he had Caracalla take his place in the quadriga. In Britain he regularly used a sedan chair to get around.

It is difficult to determine the exact circumstances of Severus' death, as the ancient historians contradict one another on a number of points. It seems that he died a natural death, on 4 February 211 in Eburacum (York). A short time before, according to Cassius Dio, he had escaped an assassination attempt by his son, Caracalla, who had had his eye on the throne for some time. The attack took place during an army march. In spite of the pain in his feet, the father rode along on horseback and not in a coach. Caracalla remained behind him, and at a certain moment he reportedly unsheathed his sword and charged at his father. He pulled back when others began yelling and warned his father. Upon hearing the shouting Septimius Severus turned around but said nothing. It was only later that he brought up the matter. In the presence of several confidants, including the commander of the imperial guard Papinianus, he laid a sword on a table before Caracalla and said, 'If you really want to kill me, then do it here. You are young and I am an old man and can hardly stand on my own two feet. If you do not dare to do it yourself, there is always Papinianus next to you, and you can order him to kill me. He will probably do whatever you ask of him, because you are in fact now already emperor.' After that Septimius Severus let the matter rest.

For the last days of his life the emperor was bedridden. Until the moment of his death Septimius Severus remained in control. In his final moments he asked for a porphyry urn. He held it up to his face and said, 'Soon you shall contain a man the world could not hold.' Just before he died he said to his two sons, 'Don't quarrel among yourselves, give the soldiers their pay and pay no heed to what others may say.' His last words were, 'I was everything, and it was all for naught.'

Septimius Severus' body was cremated in the presence of the soldiers. His ashes were put in the urn he had held in his hands and then taken to Rome and interred in the Mausoleum of Hadrian.

Cassius Dio 77.14–17
Herodian 3.15
Scriptores Historiae Augustae, *Severus* 22–24

GETA
7 March 189–end of December 211
Emperor from 4 February 211

Shortly before his death, Septimius Severus had decided that his two sons should rule jointly, but little came of that in practice because Caracalla took charge from the outset. Although his brother Geta, who, like him, bore the title Augustus, also had a valid claim to the throne, it was clear to everyone that it was the elder of the two brothers who had the initiative. In 195, when he was a lad of seven, his father was already grooming him for the emperorship. His father had given him the name Marcus Aurelius Antoninus to express solidarity with the emperors Trajan, Hadrian, Antoninus Pius and Marcus Aurelius. However he is not known by that name, but as Caracalla, since he would often wear a special Gallic cloak, the *caracalla*.

While Caracalla enjoyed the sympathy of the armies, Geta was assured of the support of his powerful mother, Julia Domna, and a number of leading senators. The brothers lived in separate wings of the imperial palace and took no notice of each other. They viewed each other with suspicion, and each tried to trump the other in acquiring the sympathy of influential people. In the end they decided to divide the Empire. Geta would have Antioch as his capital, while Caracalla would remain in Rome. But they never got this far because Caracalla soon changed his mind and decided to kill his brother.

The assassination took place on 26 December 211. Caracalla had actually wanted to get rid of his brother earlier, during the annual festival of Saturnalia, but he decided against it because a number of people were aware of the animosity between the brothers and Geta had come to the ceremonies surrounded by bodyguards. But Caracalla did not change his plans. When his mother invited both brothers for a reconciliatory talk at her home they both came unarmed and without bodyguards. However, Caracalla had taken precautions and had a number of centurions waiting in ambush. When Geta passed by, they fell upon him. He fled to his mother, and as he threw his arms around her, seeking solace on her lap, he was stabbed. His voice faltering, he whimpered, 'Mother, who did bear me, help me. I am being murdered', and thus he breathed his last in her arms. It must have been a pathetic sight, a mother covered in the blood of her dying son. But she could not cry, not in public and not in private, because Caracalla was now the sole emperor and watched her every move.

Cassius Dio 78.2
Herodian 4.4

CARACALLA
4 April 188–8 April 217
Emperor from 4 February 211

That same evening Caracalla went to the army camp and acted as if he had just escaped an assassination attempt. He promised the soldiers a pay rise. The citizens of Rome suffered greatly during this time. Caracalla knew that Geta had many friends in Rome, and he gave the order for an enormous massacre. In the first months of 212 more than twenty thousand people perished, among them a number of senators. The relationship between the emperor and the Senate was permanently soured. After dealing with his enemies, he tried to win over the populace that same year by, among other things, building a complex of thermal baths, which would later become famous. To make the deeply bureaucratised Empire more manageable and to gain insight into the national income, he granted Roman citizenship to all free male inhabitants of the Empire, a measure that entered the history books as the *Constitutio Antoniniana*. These are bright spots in a reign that was otherwise distinguished only by bloodshed.

In 213 Caracalla left Rome. He first visited Gaul and Germania, returning to Rome for a short time in the winter of 213–214 and then leaving for the east. He would not see Rome again. During his journey, in Thrace, he became fascinated by Alexander the Great, with whom he increasingly began to identify. Whenever he could, he would visit those places where his great predecessor had been, and he had double portraits made of himself and his role model. During a visit to Alexandria in the winter of 215–216 he once again displayed his inordinate cruelty and had thousands of people killed. The real purpose of his expedition was to settle old scores with the Parthians, who continually threatened the eastern border of the Empire. Profiting from the rivalry between two pretenders to the throne, the Roman troops were able to cross the Euphrates.

On 8 April 217 Caracalla's turbulent life came to an end, doubtless in a different way than he himself ever would have imagined. He had made camp with his troops in Edessa, a short distance to the east of the Euphrates, and readied himself for the coming campaigns. He was well aware that he had enemies and was always surrounded by clairvoyants and astrologers. He trusted them, followed their advice and executed people they considered to be dangerous. In his paranoia he went so far as to write a letter to Materianus, the city prefect of Rome, with the request to use clairvoyants to learn what the future had in store for him. One piece of advice was that he should watch out for Macrinus, the prefect of the imperial guard, who was often to be found in his presence. By a stroke of good fortune Macrinus happened to intercept the letter. He understood that his fate would be sealed if he did not act quickly. He took Martialis into his confidence; the latter was a centurion whose brother had been executed by Caracalla a short time before and who had himself been accused of cowardice by the emperor.

Macrinus and Martialis waited for an opportune moment. One presented itself on 8 April 217. Accompanied only by a few knights, among them Martialis, Caracalla left the army camp to make a sacrifice at the shrine of Selene in the nearby town of Carrhae. Midway through the journey he had to urinate. He dismounted and went off by himself. He had just one guard with him, who kept a respectful distance. While Caracalla was relieving himself, Martialis ran up to him as if he had something urgent to say. The emperor looked up at him and at the same moment Martialis stabbed him with a dagger just below his collarbone, probably in the heart, since Caracalla died instantly. Martialis fled, but he was caught and impaled by spears.

Macrinus took charge right away. Martialis was dead and no one suspected that there was anyone else behind the assassination. Everyone thought Martialis had acted out of vengeance. The army had rushed to the scene of the catastrophe, and Macrinus bent over the deceased emperor and wept profusely. The body of Caracalla was placed on a funeral pyre and burned. The ashes were put in an urn and sent to his mother, who was at that moment in Antioch. She was overwhelmed by profound sadness. The anguish of losing two sons, both of whom had died violent deaths, was more than she could bear. According to Herodian, after hearing the news of Caracalla's death she took her own life; Cassius Dio writes that she first tried to seize power. When she was ordered to leave Antioch she refused all food and drink and died a tragic death.

Cassius Dio 79.5–6
Herodian 4.13
Scriptores Historiae Augustae, *Antoninus Caracalla* 7

MACRINUS
c. 165–June/July 218
Emperor from 11 April 217–8 June 218

Three days after Caracalla's death the armies of the east proclaimed Macrinus emperor. He was the first non-senator to hold the supreme office. He was from Mauretania and had worked his way up through the imperial bureaucracy under Septimius Severus. Caracalla had appointed him commander of the imperial guard.

From the first day of his reign Macrinus did not have the best of luck with his decisions. He tried to reach an agreement with the

Parthian king Artabanus. The latter acted as if he were prepared to talk, but in the meantime he mobilised an army that succeeded in defeating the Romans. Macrinus was only able to extricate himself from this thorny situation by buying off the Parthians with huge sums of money. People also resented him for not returning to Rome, not even when a major fire and severe floods seriously damaged the Colosseum and the Forum. Worst of all for him was the fact that he alienated the armies by underpaying the young recruits.

A revolt against Macrinus was only a matter of time. The initiative came from Julia Maesa, Julia Domna's sister. Like her sister, she was a dynamic woman. She put forward her fourteen-year-old grandson Avitus, better known by the name Heliogabalus. Macrinus tried to turn the tide, but the few troops who remained loyal to him were defeated by Heliogabalus' forces on 8 June 218. Before the fighting started Macrinus had designated his son Diadumenianus, who was not yet ten years old, as his successor. After the battle the emperor sent him to the Parthians as an envoy to rally support. He himself tried to flee to Rome.

He must have known the game was up. Herodian and Cassius Dio detail the emperor's ignominious flight. He had taken off his cloak with the imperial insignias and shaved his beard so he would not be recognised. Like a hunted animal he fled through Cilicia, Cappadocia, Galatia and Bithynia, hoping to evade the pursuers Heliogabalus had sent. But eventually exhaustion got the better of him. In Chalcedon in Bithynia he was recognised, captured and turned over to his enemies. In Cappadocia he received the news that his son had also been taken captive, at Zeugma on the eastern border, and had been killed. At his wits' end he threw himself from the chariot in which he was being transported, but he suffered only a broken shoulder. Not long afterwards he was put to death by a centurion outside Antioch. He had been in power fourteen months.

Cassius Dio 79.39–40
Herodian 5.4
Scriptores Historiae Augustae, *Macrinus* 10, 15

HELIOGABALUS
Also known as Antoninus
c. 203/204–11 March 222
Emperor from 16 May 218

Macrinus was dead and power quickly passed to Avitus/Heliogabalus. The fact that he came to power at a young age was the work of his mother Julia Soaemias, the daughter of Julia Maesa. Both wanted to keep the throne in the family and took advantage of the young Heliogabalus. The soldiers in the east followed their lead. The Senate in Rome, afraid of the soldiers, had no choice but to accept the situation. Yet the two women had misjudged the character of the young emperor. With Heliogabalus a man ascended the throne who fitted into the tradition of perverted emperors such as Caligula, Nero, Commodus and Caracalla.

He took on the title Antoninus in an attempt to suggest that he was the son of Caracalla, but he would go down in history under the name Heliogabalus, an appellation derived from the Semitic god Elagabal (Baal), whose high priest he was in Emesa. From the start of his reign he did everything to betray the trust he enjoyed. On the way to Rome, during a stay in Nicomedia in the winter of 218–219, he presented himself as a religious figure who would bring peace and order to the Roman Empire. But this was not a message Romans were particularly eager to hear. They wanted nothing to do with his newfangled ideas. The black stone from the temple in Emesa that he brought along to Rome elicited only disgust. It was bad enough that he built a temple to the god Elagabal on the Palatine and forced the senators to witness him in his capacity as a high priest worshipping the stone as a divine force, but when he elevated his god above the Roman god Jupiter he had crossed the line.

In his private life he went even further. He married three women and one man and had numerous lovers of both sexes. His decision to marry a vestal virgin enraged the Romans. The vestal virgins were considered paragons of purity and decency. The violation of her virginity was regarded by the Romans as an affront to their entire religion.

While Heliogabalus traipsed from one orgy to another, it was his grandmother and mother who were the real power behind the throne. But Heliogabalus' eccentric behaviour drove the two women apart. Julia Maesa saw that opposition to her grandson was on the rise. She washed her hands of him and backed another grandson, Alexianus, who would later take the name Severus Alexander. He was just thirteen years old. Heliogabalus was forced to accept his cousin as Caesar. On 26 June 221 the adoption took place, but the relationship between the eccentric Heliogabalus and the unassuming Severus Alexander was hardly one of harmonious co-operation. It was clear that one of them would have to step aside.

Heliogabalus knew he would die a violent death. That had once been predicted by Syrian priests. Therefore he had purple or satin-wrapped nooses, golden swords and jewel-encrusted jars of poison at the ready throughout his palace. He also had a high tower built from which he could throw himself; below were sheets of gold inlaid with gemstones. His death, he remarked to his few friends, must be expensive and lavish. But he was sorely mistaken.

In the spring of 222 the situation came to a head. Heliogabalus, together with his mother, tried to get rid of Severus Alexander, but their attempts ended in failure, mainly because his grandmother had made sure that his cousin was well protected. Heliogabalus then put out the story that Severus Alexander was seriously ill and near death. The soldiers of the imperial guard did not accept this and demanded to see him. Heliogabalus had no choice but to bow to their wishes. He must have felt very uncomfortable when he was taken to the soldiers' camp along with his mother and Severus Alexander. The latter was greeted with cheers, while Heliogabalus was jeered at and mocked. He flew into a rage and railed at the soldiers for the rest of the night. But by then they no longer cared what he thought.

Towards morning Heliogabalus began to lose his grip on the situation. The soldiers pressed closer and closer to him and seemed to be on the point of storming the camp shrine in which he had taken shelter. Heliogabalus hoped to smuggle himself out in a coffin. But the soldiers knew no mercy. They forced their way into the shrine and found the eighteen-year-old boy-emperor in the arms of his mother. Both of them were put to the sword. The author of this story in the *Historia Augusta* has a somewhat different version of events: Heliogabalus had hidden in a toilet but was dragged out by the soldiers and killed. The bodies of the emperor and his mother were carried triumphantly through the city, gruesomely mutilated and eventually thrown into the sewer that led into the Tiber. But because the pipes were too narrow, the corpses were weighted down with stones and tossed off a bridge.

So hated was Heliogabalus that the soldiers did not want to take the risk that his body might float to the surface and be reclaimed for burial.

Cassius Dio 80.19–21
Herodian 5.8
Scriptores Historiae Augustae, *Antoninus Heliogabalus* 15–18, 33

SEVERUS ALEXANDER
1 October 208–February/March 235
Emperor from 13 March 222

The Senate was so glad to be rid of Heliogabalus that Severus Alexander was granted not only the highest rank, but also the title *Pater patriae* ('father of the country'). Just like his predecessor he was only fourteen years old when he came to power and, like him, he stood in the shadow of a dominant mother, Julia Mamaea, who was never far away from her son. She made sure her son did what she wanted. Because Severus Alexander was so modest and submissive she was able to leave her mark on his reign. People whose influence on the emperor was too great knew that they would have to answer to her. One person who found this out was Orbiana, a descendant of an old patrician family. She was the emperor's wife, but when Severus Alexander gave her the title Augusta his mother seethed with jealousy. Orbiana was banished, and her father was killed.

Severus Alexander's meddlesome mother prevented him from ever becoming popular with the troops. He was not a soldier himself, nor did he feel any particular affinity for military life. On the eastern border of the Empire Severus Alexander was confronted with the emergent nationalism of the Persians. Under the leadership of King Ardashir they had invaded Mesopotamia in 230 and were now threatening Syria. Severus Alexander was slow to react to the threat, and the armies did not appreciate this. He had considerable difficulty dispatching rivals who had been proclaimed emperor by the dissatisfied soldiers. As a result of this he was not able to open a front against the Persians until 232. Ardashir retreated and the status quo was restored.

However, Severus Alexander had no time to relax. He had only just returned to Rome and held a triumphal precession on 25 September in honour of his 'victory' over the Persians when he received reports that there were serious problems on the Rhine border. Germanic tribes had crossed the Rhine and were wreaking havoc. In 235 it seemed as if Severus Alexander was going to confront the enemy on the battlefield, but to the soldiers' dismay he merely bought off the Germans. This, combined with his decision to ignore their calls for higher pay, permanently alienated them from him.

Severus Alexander had always been convinced that the soldiers would remain loyal to him in the end. He had systematically ignored omens that predicted that his life was in danger. But things did not turn out the way he had hoped. In the early spring of 235 the army was bivouacked at two camps near Mainz. The soldiers in the one camp turned on him and offered the emperorship to Maximinus, a Thracian of peasant stock who had worked his way up through the ranks to become general. After a brief and probably feigned hesitation Maximinus accepted the imperial title and took immediate action. At the head of an army he ventured forth to the camp where Severus Alexander was staying; also in the camp were his mother, his bodyguards and a large number of soldiers. Severus Alexander panicked when the news of the coup reached him. He ran out of his tent, crying and trembling over his entire body. He reproached Maximinus for his disloyalty and ingratitude after everything he had done for him and admonished the soldiers for violating their oath of allegiance.

For a time it seemed as if the soldiers in his own camp would continue to support him. But when early the next day a thick cloud of dust announced the arrival of Maximinus' forces, they abandoned him, blaming his mother Julia Mamaea for the depleted treasury and their inadequate pay. They left the camp in droves and joined up with Maximinus. Severus Alexander retreated to his tent and waited for the inevitable. His arms wrapped around his mother, he kept repeating that it was her fault that everything had gone wrong. Not long afterwards, mother and son were found and killed.

With the death of Severus Alexander the dynasty of the African and Syrian emperors, which had governed the Roman Empire for almost forty-two years, came to an end. His body was brought to Rome and interred in a magnificent tomb. Three years later he was even deified at the behest of the Senate. This was really not all that surprising. Severus Alexander was a thoughtful ruler, with a sense of the traditional Roman values, whose greatest mistake was probably his inability to break free of the will of his mother.

Herodian 6.8–9
Scriptores Historiae Augustae, *Alexander Severus* 60–62
Aurelius Victor, *Liber de Caesaribus* 24
Eutropius 6.2

6

THE SOLDIER EMPERORS

Maximinus the Thracian is the kind of emperor who dominated the third century: a career soldier, unencumbered by any loyalty to the Senate. His reign marks the beginning of a period in which the weaknesses of the Roman Empire, which until then could to some extent be papered over, became visible. This period of crisis, during which the armies called the shots, putting forward their commanders as new emperors, lasted fifty years. It was an age of violence. With a single exception every one of the soldier emperors met a violent end. Not one of them was able to stop the decline. The Empire sank deeper and deeper into a morass of political, military, economic and financial problems.

The question has often been asked how things had been allowed to reach this point, how it was possible that the stable Empire of the first two centuries had fallen so far in a space of fifty years. To this day there is no generally accepted explanation for the crisis of the third century, which is not surprising, given the complexity of the problems. The most disparate reasons have been proposed to explain the decline: the moral laxity of the citizens of a welfare state, the loss of the old Roman virtues, a drop in population as a result of the Persian and German invasions, civil wars, the government's inept financial policies, the high cost of maintaining the armies, a widening rift between the urban bourgeoisie and the peasants, who could count on the support of the armies, and the fact that Roman society was unable to increase production.

If one thing has become clear from the scholarly debate of the last few decades, it is that none of the aforementioned causes led to the crisis on its own. It was a combination of factors interacting with one another, with the rapidly worsening military situation on the borders acting, in the view of most scholars, as a catalyst.

Throughout the third century barbaric tribes, lured by the prosperity of the Roman Empire, tried to cross the borders: from southern

Germany the Alamanni, from Hungary the Vandals, from southern Russia the Goths, on the eastern border the Persians and on the southern borders of the African provinces various nomadic tribes. The Goths and the Persians in particular penetrated deep into the Empire with great regularity.

Even though the army was not very successful in fighting off the invaders, the status of soldiers remained unaffected. The emperors were aware that the continued existence of the Roman Empire was dependent on a well-functioning army. But at the same time they realised that their own position was dependent on the strength and loyalty of the troops. Pay rises, better living conditions in the army camps and the promise of career opportunities upon returning to civilian life were the pledges they had to make in order to assure themselves of the soldiers' support.

Even so, the customary recruitment drives in the heartland of the Roman Empire yielded an insufficient number of soldiers, and the authorities were increasingly forced to appeal to 'barbarians' from the outlying provinces, where the standard of living was lower and the influence of the incursions was most apparent. This resulted in a barbarisation of the army and a decreased sense of solidarity with Rome. The soldiers knew very well that they were indispensable to the emperors and acted accordingly. They made ever greater financial demands, and if these were not met they had no qualms about backing a rival candidate.

The high costs of maintaining the armies slowed economic development. Production and trade declined. The consequence was that a smaller number of people were forced to shoulder a greater fiscal burden, a state of affairs that led to tax evasion. To ensure that taxes were paid, the authorities created a new division of the civil service, which used strong-arm tactics to force people into paying their share. But because the officials were not immune to corruption, the system did not work and there was a continual shortage of money.

Following that, the government resorted to coining large amounts of new money. The new coins had a lower silver content than the old ones, and were thus worth less and were scarcely accepted by the populace. The inflation reached such heights that confidence in the value of money completely disappeared.

Taxpayer morale within the Empire was at a low ebb, and many tried to shirk the oppressive fiscal obligations. In many regions people bypassed money and engaged in bartering. The state's attempts to tighten its grip on its citizenry and increase the amount of money in circulation by further devaluing the currency backfired. In order for the government to obtain the needed money, the notables of the imperial cities were held personally responsible for shortfalls in their cities and had to make up the difference out of their own pockets. Many ducked out of this obligation, left the cities and withdrew to their landholdings, where they set up a kind of private economy. They were outside the grasp of the tax collectors, and as a result the cities sank into poverty and employment opportunities dried up, a development that had disastrous consequences, particularly for the lower classes. For small-time farmers the situation was hardly rosier. No longer able to make a profit from their activities, they abandoned their farms and placed themselves under the protection of the large landholders as tenant farmers. However bad their position there was, they were at least guaranteed a modicum of economic and social security. If the situation there also deteriorated, banditry offered a chance to escape that life. Thus the third century saw the emergence of large gangs of disappointed ex-farmers prowling the countryside.

GORDIAN I
158/159–20 January 238
Emperor from early January 238

GORDIAN II
192–20 January 238
Emperor from early January 238

Ancient historians claim that the first of the soldier emperors, Maximinus the Thracian, was of very humble origins. It is said his parents were peasants in a village in Thrace and that for a time he himself earned a living as a shepherd. The stories about his great height and tremendous physical strength are legion. According to the undoubtedly exaggerated description in the *Historia Augusta* he was taller than two and a half metres. His fingers were so thick that he wore one of his wife's bracelets as a ring. Without the help of draft animals he would pull carts filled with heavy loads. In short: his physical capabilities seemed almost limitless.

Maximinus' position was never secure, though he might have thought it was when he gave his son the title of Caesar and had his late wife deified. The Senate reluctantly agreed to his appointment, but soon there were coups, in which a number of senators were also involved. These coups were thwarted, however, and for a short time Maximinus had a free hand to drive back the Germans and secure the borders. These campaigns on the borders were extremely costly, and the result was a substantial tax increase. And this was not exactly conducive to the emperor's popularity among senators, knights and provincial administrators, who were responsible for the lion's share of the taxes.

The situation became quite complex in the early days of 238. The population of north Africa opposed the high taxes and proclaimed Gordian, the eighty-year-old proconsul of the province Africa, emperor. The Senate recognised the appointment at once. After all he was one of them, and nothing like the uncivilised Maximinus. Together with his son of the same name he went to war against Maximinus. But the plans of father and son came to grief almost immediately because they were unable to raise an army of trained soldiers. When Capellianus, the governor of Numidia, who had remained loyal to Maximinus, advanced on them with his army, the groups of hastily recruited soldiers, armed only with sticks, clubs and knives, were no match for Capellianus' well-trained men. Gordian II perished in the fighting; his body was never found. His father, who had not taken part in the battle on account of his age, retired to his room after hearing the disastrous news, to get some rest, he said. He strangled himself with his belt. The co-emperorship of father and son had lasted just a few weeks.

Herodian 7.9
Scriptores Historiae Augustae, *The Two Maximi* 23–24

MAXIMINUS THE THRACIAN
172/173–April 238
Emperor from February/March 235

The senators were panic-stricken. They knew that Maximinus would soon turn his attention to Italy and realised that there was no reason to hope for clemency. They selected two ex-consuls of advanced age from their own ranks, Balbinus and Pupienus, and appointed them emperors.

A confrontation between the newly appointed emperors and Maximinus, who was advancing towards Italy, was inevitable. But before things got that far, Maximinus was given a painful signal that his power in the Empire was on the wane. When he came to call at the city of Aquileia to let his exhausted soldiers rest and stock up on provisions after crossing the Alps, he found the gates closed. He decided to lay siege to the city, but the inhabitants mounted a spirited defence. Supplies started running low and morale plummeted. The soldiers of the Second Parthian Legion, which had its home base on the mountain of Alba near Rome, had had enough and decided to kill the emperor. It was the middle of the day, and there was a lull in the fighting. Most of the soldiers had returned to their quarters, as had Emperor Maximinus. The rebellious soldiers of the legions walked to his tent and tore his image off the military standards. Remarkably enough they were aided by the emperor's bodyguards, probably because, like them, the soldiers were from Italy and had come to the realisation that they were protecting an emperor who was hated in their homeland. Upon hearing the commotion Maximinus and his son came out and tried to calm the soldiers. But they were unmoved by his arguments and stabbed him. The dead bodies of Maximinus and his son were deposited in the centre of camp, where they were trampled on and left behind as garbage. The two heads were sent on to Rome.

Herodian 8.5–6
Scriptores Historiae Augustae, *The Two Maximi* 23–24

PUPIENUS
c. 164–early May 238
Emperor from late January 238

BALBINUS
?–early May 238
Emperor from late January 238

Maximinus' death solved nothing. Pupienus and Balbinus did not act in concert, even though we can see many texts on the coins minted during their brief reign that make reference to harmony. They hated each other and neither was willing to take a back seat to the other. They had never been popular with the soldiers, certainly not with the soldiers of the imperial guard, who found it hard to take the fact that the emperors' German bodyguards were given preferential treatment. During the Capitoline festival the situation came to a head. Afraid that they were going to be removed from their posts, the soldiers of the guard marched on the imperial palace, determined to kill the emperors. In what would be their final hour Pupienus and Balbinus could not agree on how to deal with the rebellious guardsmen. The former wanted to deploy the German guard against them, but the latter thought that it was a ruse dreamt up by his colleague to get rid of him.

While they were arguing, the soldiers stormed the palace. They grabbed both emperors, tore off their garments and dragged them out of the palace. They pulled out their hair, eyebrows and beards, beat, punched, kicked and stabbed them, but they made sure to do all this in such a way that their deaths would be long and painful. Only when the German bodyguards got wind of what was happening and readied themselves for a counter-attack were the emperors killed. Their badly mutilated bodies were left on the street. The soldiers proclaimed Gordian III, the thirteen-year-old grandson of Gordian I, emperor. Then they withdrew to their camp with the new emperor. The German bodyguards elected not to take any further action.

Herodian 8.8

Scriptores Historiae Augustae, *Maximus and Balbinus* 13–14

GORDIAN III
20 January 225–February 244
Emperor from January/February 238

The choice of Gordian III had the approval of the Senate, the people and the soldiers. He had the good fortune to have an able adviser in Timesitheus, whom he himself had appointed commander of the imperial guard shortly after ascending the throne. In the nearly six years that he wielded power there was relative calm, certainly in comparison with the years preceding and following his rule. The problems he faced were caused by the Persian king Shapur, who had succeeded his father Ardashir. He had crossed the border and taken control of portions of Roman territory, but in 243 he was defeated by the Romans at the battle of Rhesaina (northern Mesopotamia).

That same year saw the death of Timesitheus, the man who had led the campaign up to that point. His place was taken by Philip, who would become known under the name Philip the Arab. For Gordian this was the beginning of the end.

To everyone around him it was clear that Philip had imperial aspirations. He made up all sorts of stories to discredit Gordian, and people believed them. The soldiers in the army camp in Ctesiphon, not far from the Euphrates, who had been suffering from disruptions in the grain deliveries, began to believe the rumours he had been fabricating and repeated his contention that Gordian was unfit to reign and that only a strong hand could lead the Empire. In the end Philip managed to get himself elected co-regent. Gordian increasingly found himself on the defensive and had to surrender his powers to Philip one by one. In the end it all got to be too much for him. He climbed on to a platform and tried to explain to the soldiers why there was a food shortage in the army camps: it was all Philip's fault; it was he who had been deliberately diverting the grain ships. In his despair he asked the soldiers whom they wanted to be emperor, him or Philip. He took a gamble and lost. The soldiers rejected him. His fate was sealed, since Philip realised that as long as Gordian was in the army camp, his own position was vulnerable. Therefore he decided to get rid of him. Gordian was led away under fierce protests; his imperial robe and decorations were stripped from him, and after that he was murdered. Philip did not want it to leak out right away that he was responsible for the emperor's death. He sent a message to the Senate saying that Gordian has succumbed to an illness and that he himself had subsequently been proclaimed emperor by the army. He achieved the desired result. The Senate accepted his version of events, and he became the official emperor of the Roman Empire.

Philip agreed to have Gordian's remains brought to Rome for burial. In the end he was even deified.

Scriptores Historiae Augustae, *The Three Gordiani* 29–31

PHILIP THE ARAB
c. 204–September/October 249
Emperor from February 244

After the death of Gordian information about the emperors becomes even spottier. The writings of Herodian, a source that later writers relied on extensively, are sorely missed here. Even in the *Historia Augusta* a number of emperors are absent, among them Philip and his successor Decius. We have to make do with such authors as Aurelius Victor, Lactantius, Eusebius and Zosimus, who have relatively little to say about the time of the soldier emperors.

Philip was born in a small town in the Roman province of Arabia, which he later named Philippolis after himself. Not much is known about his family beyond the fact that his father was a Roman citizen and his brother had held the rank of prefect of the imperial guard before him. Shortly after assuming power Philip was confronted with rapidly mounting pressure on the Danube borders, which was the reason he made peace with King Shapur after being appointed, a decision that cost him five hundred thousand denarii. In 246–247 he waged war on the German tribes along the Danube. He considered himself to be the victor, and in the autumn of 247 he held a triumphal procession in Rome. In April 248 he attended the grand festivities commemorating the thousand-year anniversary of the founding of the city.

A year later Philip was dead. The troops on the Danube felt that the emperor had not met enough of their demands and rose up against him at an extremely inopportune moment. Their revolt coincided with renewed activity by Germanic tribes, especially the Goths. Philip declared in the Senate that if it was in the interest of Rome for him to abdicate, he would do so at once. Eventually a senator, Decius by name, took the floor and stated that the leader of the rebels, Pacatianus, lacked sufficient support to pose any real danger. He was proved right, for shortly thereafter Pacatianus was killed by his own soldiers. But the threat of new pretenders to the throne remained. In Cappadocia, Jotapianus proclaimed himself emperor. He had coins minted with his likeness but was soon killed by the same soldiers who had backed his candidacy. Uranius, who had proclaimed himself emperor in Syria, would meet the same fate.

Because the Goths continued to threaten the Danube provinces, Philip was forced to take action. He could have gone to the endangered area himself, but he chose to put the senator Decius in charge instead. Initially it looked as if he had made the right choice, since the enemy was defeated, but what was to follow was less pleasant for him: in June 249 Decius was proclaimed emperor by the armies, a strange twist of fate, considering that a year earlier that same Decius had told the Senate that Philip had no cause to worry about rival emperors since they did not stand a chance.

The only thing Philip could do was to raise an army to fight Decius and confront his rival on the battlefield. Far from Rome, near Beroa in Macedonia – according to other accounts near Verona in northern Italy – the two armies met in September or October 249. To be sure, it was Philip who had the larger army, but Decius' soldiers were full of self-confidence from the victories of the previous year and were prepared to give their lives for their general. From the beginning of the battle the balance tipped in Decius' favour. Philip's troops were massacred, and Philip himself was also killed in battle. His twelve-year-old son Philip, whom he had appointed Caesar, was probably slain as well, although according to other accounts he stayed behind in Rome and was murdered there by the soldiers of the imperial guard when they heard the news of his father's defeat. For Decius it was not enough that Philip was dead. All trace of him was wiped out. His name was obliterated from all honorary inscriptions.

Zosimus 1.21–22
Aurelius Victor, *Liber de Caesaribus* 28

DECIUS
c. 190–June 251
Emperor from September/October 249

Of the emperors who led the Roman Empire in the turbulent years 235–285, Decius is the best known. He does not owe this distinction to his policies or his military accomplishments, but to the systematic persecutions of Christians that he organised. In the two years that this ex-consul of Balkan birth was on the throne he tried to stem the growing influence of Christianity, this was reason enough for later Christian writers to portray him as a bad emperor in every respect. It is hard to say if their judgement was correct. Decius was not in power long enough to be able to make any real policy. Moreover for a large part of his reign he was off leading military campaigns, particularly in the Danube lands against the Goths. Under the leadership of their king Kniva, who possessed great military talents, they pressed ahead time and again. Decius and Kniva would fight many a battle.

In 251, in the middle of the fight against the Goths, Decius' life came to a tragic end. After repeated skirmishes with varying outcomes the Goths had destroyed the city of Philippopolis in Thrace and were in the process of retreating, rich with the plunder they had collected. In the area around the mouth of the Danube Decius tried to cut them off. Gallus, the governor of Moesia, was supposed to help him out by sending troops. The idea was to use the two armies to corner the Goths, but things did not turn out as he had planned. Gallus proved to be less trustworthy than Decius had thought, at least according to the writer Zosimus, who provides the most in-depth account of the battle. Gallus sent messengers to the Goths inviting them to take part in a coup against Decius. The Goths probably accepted this offer; they positioned themselves in three divisions opposite Decius' troops at a spot where they (and presumably Gallus as well) knew that there would be a vast swamp between the two armies. The place was called Abrittus. Considering the geographic condition of the terrain, it seems inconceivable that Decius would have chosen this place spontaneously. Could it have been at the prompting of the treacherous Gallus? There is scarcely any other explanation. Nevertheless Decius managed to defeat two of the three divisions of the Goth army and then set about pursuing the final division. Without considering the dangers of a pursuit through a swamp, the Romans went after the Goths. They got stuck in the mud and were unable to move. As they sank deeper and deeper, the Goths shot their arrows at the thousands of helpless Romans. Decius and his son Herennius Etruscus, who had been appointed Augustus shortly before the battle, were among the victims. Their bodies were never found. It was one of the worst defeats ever suffered by the Romans, comparable to the defeat of Varus by the Germans in the Teutoburger Wald in AD 9 and the battle of Cannae in 216 BC, which they lost to the Carthaginians. Decius was the first emperor to die in battle against enemies from outside the Empire.

Because he had been a good emperor in the eyes of the Senate, he was deified, but that did nothing to diminish the memory of his inglorious end.

Zosimus 1.23
Lactantius, *On the Death of the Persecutors* 4

TREBONIANUS GALLUS
c. 206–August 253
Emperor from June 251

Trebonianus Gallus was proclaimed emperor by the troops. We know nothing about his past besides the fact that he came from an old Etruscan family. Shortly after acceding to office he made peace with the Goths, who were allowed to keep the plunder and the Roman prisoners of war, and returned to Rome. There he did something remarkable, certainly in light of the treason he was suspected of committing: he adopted Decius' son Hostilian and made him co-emperor. But Hostilian died that same year, probably of the plague, which was then raging in Rome. Gallus subsequently made his own son Volusianus emperor.

The two years that Gallus wielded the sceptre were hardly trouble-free. Shapur was again making bellicose noises in the east, invading the province of Syria and capturing the capital Antioch. There was little that Gallus could do about it. The Goths had again crossed the Danube border and were running riot on Roman territory. Aemilian, an ex-consul from Tunisia, succeeded in putting a stop to this. He promptly raised an army and defeated the invaders, committing a bloodbath in the process. He then drove the remnants of the Gothic army back across the Danube and laid waste to their homelands.

The soldiers were deeply devoted to Aemilian. They saw him as a Roman commander of the old style who led his troops from victory to victory, and they subsequently proclaimed him emperor. Aemilian was not immune to their enthusiasm. He assumed command of a large army and headed for Italy to depose Gallus. In great haste Gallus took countermeasures. Messengers were sent to the Rhine border to summon Valerian, the commander of the Rhine legion, to Italy with his troops. But before he could get there Gallus and Aemilian had fought out their conflict. The setting was Interamna, approximately eighty kilometres north of Rome. Gallus' soldiers quickly realised that they were outnumbered and that their opponents, buoyed by their recent victories over the Goths, were in a winning mood. They turned against their emperor and killed both him and his son, firmly convinced that the new emperor would reward them handsomely.

Jordanes, *Getica* 105–106
Aurelius Victor, *Liber de Caesaribus* 31
Zosimus 1.28

AEMILIAN
c. 207–September/October 253
Emperor from July/August 253

Aemilian was now emperor, but not for long. *En route* to Italy Valerian learned of the death of Gallus and was proclaimed emperor by his troops. That news also reached the army camp of Aemilian. The soldiers, who had been so enthusiastic about Aemilian just a short time before, now abandoned him and killed him, either because he was not paying them enough or because they had more trust in Valerian. According to Aurelius Victor, Aemilian did not die a violent death, but succumbed to disease. His reign had lasted less than three months.

Aurelius Victor, *Liber de Caesaribus* 31
Zosimus 1.29

VALERIAN
c. 195–after 260
Emperor from June/August 253

Valerian was fifty-eight when he became emperor in the summer of 253. A few months later the senators heartily endorsed his candidacy, happy that someone from an old senatorial family was now in charge. They also agreed to the appointment of his son Gallienus as co-emperor. Although they formed a good couple they did not have an easy time of it, because there were wars to be fought in both the west and the east. Gallienus was given the task of protecting Gaul and the Rhine border from incursions by the Germanic tribes. Despite incidental successes he could not prevent the Franks from entering northern Spain and destroying the city of Tarraco (Tarragona). Meanwhile his father was in the east, where he put down a revolt led by Uranius Antoninus and reconquered Antioch from the Persian king Shapur.

But it was that same Shapur who saw to it that Valerian met what is perhaps the most degrading end of all Roman emperors. According to Lactantius in his book *On the Death of the Persecutors*, Valerian's death was God's vengeance for the anti-Christian persecutions he initiated. It all started in 260. Valerian was trying to defend the city of Edessa from attacks by the Persians. The soldiers were having a tough time, because their ranks had been thinned out by the plague. Valerian sensed that the situation was becoming precarious, and in June or July he sent envoys to Shapur to discuss the conditions of a truce. The Persian king replied that he would only discuss the matter with the emperor personally. Valerian agreed to this request and met Shapur, accompanied by only a few bodyguards. While they were exchanging ideas Persian soldiers suddenly grabbed Valerian and led him away.

According to Lactantius, Valerian became the object of Persian scorn. Shapur took him along with him everywhere. Whenever the king wanted to get into his chariot or mount his horse he ordered the emperor to bow before him and offer him his back, so he could use him as a step. Time and again he would bark at him that this was reality, not the victories depicted on the Roman frescos. Even after Valerian died in captivity, the humiliations did not end. His skin was stripped from his body, dyed a deep red and hung in a Persian temple. And whenever Roman emissaries were visiting, they were cajoled into entering the temple where the flayed skin hung, a silent testament to the greatest indignity to which a Roman emperor had ever been subjected.

Lactantius, *On the Death of the Persecutors* 5
Aurelius Victor, *Liber de Caesaribus* 32
Zosimus 1.36

GALLIENUS
c. 213–September 268
Emperor from September/October 253

Gallienus was forty when his father named him co-emperor. Seven years later his father disappeared into Persian captivity and he was left to fend for himself. The problems he had to contend with were great. The situation on the border remained volatile, and pretenders to the throne were popping up throughout the Empire. The sources mention the names of various interested parties who attempted to seize power. The first was Ingenuus, the governor of Pannonia and Moesia. After his attempted coup was foiled, Regalianus decided to have a go at it. He too had to pay for his failure with his life, as did the candidates who followed: Macrianus and Quietus, two brothers who led a rebellion in the east but were eventually defeated. The most serious threat came from Postumus, the commander of the Rhine Army. He managed to seal off large parts of Gaul, Germania and Britain and defended the autonomy of his 'Empire' for almost ten years. Even Palmyra, which was close to the eastern border, became effectively autonomous. King Odenathus nominally reigned under the supervision of Gallienus; in reality he acted as an independent monarch.

The ancient authors are none too positive in their assessment of Gallienus' reign. They blame him for the fact that although his reign started off well, things took a turn for the worse and gradually went downhill, only to end in disaster. He allegedly abandoned himself to his love of luxury, neglecting his governmental and military duties in the arms of Pipa, the daughter of a German military commander. From an economic perspective Rome was at a low point. That said, it is sometimes forgotten that Gallienus always managed to see off the threats of new pretenders to the throne. Also overlooked is his complete overhaul of the army. The cavalry was given a much more prominent place than it had previously had, a reform that would work out well in the long run.

The year 268 was to be a fateful one for Gallienus. It began with a war against the Heruli and the Goths, who had penetrated into the Balkans and had even sacked Athens. Gallienus defeated the invaders in a great battle at Naissus in the province of Moesia. But shortly thereafter he was forced to leave the front after receiving news that the high commander of the cavalry, Aureolus, had risen up against him in Milan and had sided with Postumus. He reached Milan and defeated Aureolus just outside the city walls. The latter then retreated behind the walls and Gallienus laid siege to the city. It seemed that Gallienus had everything under control and it would only be a matter of time before order could be restored, but then a rebellion broke out within his own camp. The reason is not entirely clear, but in all probability Heraclianus, the commander of the imperial guard, felt that Claudius, who was, after Gallienus, number two in the Roman hierarchy and had earned his spurs in the military, would make a better emperor. Aurelian, the head of the cavalry after Aureolus' betrayal, Marcian, a general during the Gothic Wars, and Cecropius, leader of a division of Dalmatian knights, were also involved in the plot. They all had an Illyrian background.

Cecropius was the first to take action. When the emperor was at dinner he informed him that Aureolus and his troops had ventured out of the besieged Milan and were on their way to Gallienus' camp. The conspirators who were present at the table feigned agitation. Gallienus immediately asked for his armour, mounted his horse and called upon the soldiers to follow him. He found out too late that the story was false and Aureolus' army was nowhere to be found. The only people out there were his murderers. They rushed at him and killed him. Cecropius is said to have administered the *coup de grâce* with his lance.

Gallienus' body was brought to Rome and entombed along the Via Appia.

Scriptores Historiae Augustae, *Gallienus* 14
Aurelius Victor, *Liber de Caesaribus* 33
Zosimus 1.40

CLAUDIUS GOTHICUS
10 May 214–September 270
Emperor from September/October 268

Claudius was the first of three Illyrian emperors succeeded in temporarily bringing the Roman Empire out of its rut. His background is obscure. We know virtually nothing about his earliest past. As a soldier he had held all ranks in the army. The sources speak of his great physical strength and cruelty. It is said that he once knocked the teeth out of a horse's mouth with one punch, and in the 250s he performed as a wrestler for a time. When an opponent grabbed him by the testicles during a match, he allegedly also rendered him toothless with a single blow. But his past, which was rather unsavoury in the eyes of traditional Romans, did not prevent him from growing into an emperor who was popular not only with the soldiers, but also with the Senate and the people of Rome during his two-year reign.

The first thing he did after being proclaimed emperor was to continue the siege of Milan and force Aureolus to surrender. The rebel was executed immediately. The defence of the borders had his permanent attention. He understood that only a well-organised and disciplined army was capable of responding to the dangers of invading nations. The Alamanni, who had pushed into northern Italy, were driven back. The same thing happened to the Goths, who had taken control of large parts of the Balkans. They were routed and Claudius was given the honorary title 'Gothicus'.

Fortunately for Claudius the problems in the western part of the Empire were manageable. Postumus, who had founded his own Roman state in Gaul, met a tragic end in 269. After a victory over Laelianus, who had proclaimed himself emperor in Mainz, Postumus forbade his troops to sack the city. The soldiers, whom he had led to many victories, took exception to his order and murdered him. With Postumus the threat of an 'empire within an empire' disappeared, because Marius, a former weapon-smith who had proclaimed himself his successor, was killed after just three days by a soldier who had once worked in his smithy and had been discharged by him. Victorinus, who tried it after him, did not fare much better. To be sure, he was a capable soldier and enjoyed the sympathy of his soldiers, but his lecherousness proved to be his undoing. He assaulted the wife of one of his officers and was killed by her husband. This was in early 271.

Claudius did not live to see all this, however. In the late summer of 270 he died in Sirmium in the Balkans, where he was making preparations for a final assault on the Goths. Despite various defeats they had managed to recover and were readying themselves for new attacks on Roman territory. In all probability Claudius died a natural death, the victim of a contagious disease, which spread like wildfire and claimed many lives. It was probably a form of the plague. Aurelius Victor's suggestion that Claudius had deliberately sought death in a battle against the Goths, because the sibylline books had made this a condition for victory, does not seem terribly credible.

The announcement of his death was greeted with great sorrow in the army camp. But not only there; the Senate mourned his death as well, for with the death of Claudius an emperor disappeared who had treated the Senate with respect, without damaging his own prestige as emperor, in so far as that was possible during that turbulent century. The Senate deified him and had a gold statue of him erected on the Capitol. A golden shield bearing Claudius' likeness was placed in the Senate.

Scriptores Historiae Augustae, *Claudius* 11–12
Aurelius Victor, *Liber de Caesaribus* 34
Zosimus 1.46

QUINTILLUS
?–September 270
Emperor from September 270

It was expected that Aurelian would be Claudius' successor. He had been involved in the coup that had cost Gallienus his life. He had a reputation as a man of action and had played a leading role in the Gothic Wars. But the senators were afraid that he would not adequately protect their interests and instead chose Claudius' brother Quintillus, who at that moment was the commander of the army in northern Italy. When the soldiers in the army camp in Aquileia proclaimed Quintillus emperor, they endorsed the choice. But although Quintillus did his best to make his influence felt – for example by having numerous coins bearing his image put into circulation – it was soon clear that his reign would not be a long one. He was unable to maintain discipline in the army. In Sirmium the Danube legions proclaimed Aurelian emperor. For a short time there were two emperors. But because Quintillus could not motivate his troops to fight Aurelian, his downfall was only a matter of time.

Quintillus was not in power for long, at most a month and probably no longer than seventeen days. There are also differing opinions about his death. Some historians write that the soldiers in Aquileia turned on him and stabbed him to death with their swords. Another version is that he took his own life. There were also those who maintained that in his desperation he ordered his personal physician to open his veins and let him die a traditional Roman death.

Scriptores Historiae Augustae, *Aurelianus* 37
Zosimus 1.47

AURELIAN
9 September 214–September/October 275
Emperor from September 270

Aurelian was, like many of his predecessors, of humble origins. He was born in Illyria to a family of peasants, although his mother was said to be a priestess of the sun god. This story was probably put out later, when the sun god became the most important deity for Aurelian. He appears to have been an exemplary soldier, who stood out from his fellow soldiers even at a young age because of his great qualities. He subsequently rose through the ranks of the army. In 268, two years before he became emperor, he had already been a candidate for the office, but that time the honour went to Claudius.

Once invested with the imperial rank he had to take immediate action because the situation on the northern border had become critical thanks to the Jutungi, the Marcomanni and the Vandals. The invaders had managed to get as far as the Po Valley before they could be driven back. But Aurelian was so alarmed that in 271 he decided to fortify Rome with a large wall. This wall would be completed by later emperors.

During his reign Aurelian had to deal with a number of rivals, such as Tetricus, who believed that he could reign over his own Gallic Empire just as Postumus had done before. Together with his son of the same name he managed to hold out for nearly three years, but in 274 it was all over for him, though Aurelian did spare the lives of father and son, even giving them senior government positions. He also put an end to the ambitions of Queen Zenobia of Palmyra, so that by the beginning of 275 unity seemed to have been restored to the Empire. He took the title *Restitutor orbis* ('restorer of unity in the world'). Everything seemed to suggest that Aurelian was in complete control of things. He was even able to work on bolstering the economy through comprehensive currency reforms.

But for an emperor of the third century, danger was always lurking just around the corner, even when he thought he was firmly in the saddle. In the spring of 275 Aurelian marched eastward through Thrace to wage war on the Persians, who were once again on the move. Even before he could cross the Bosporus at Byzantium he met his end, at Caenofrurium in September or October 275. It was not a conspiracy of soldiers, praetorian guardsmen or senators that ended his life, but the machinations of a freedman. His name was Mnestheus, at least according to the *Historia Augusta*. Zosimus calls him Eros ('Love'). He was in charge of publishing imperial decrees. For reasons unknown to us the freedman had fallen into disfavour. Afraid that his days were numbered, he hatched a diabolical plan. He put together a list of people whom he believed were under surveillance by the emperor. But he also included the names of people who were not being watched. Finally he added his own name to the list. He acted as if the list had been drawn up by the emperor personally and showed it to a few people whom he had placed on it. It had the desired effect. The people who had plotted against the emperor flew into a panic; those who had done nothing wrong got angry. Without wondering if the information was reliable, they decided to take the law into their own hands. When Aurelian left the city, accompanied by only a few bodyguards, they charged at him with their swords drawn and killed him.

The soldiers could hardly believe that their beloved emperor had been killed. In deep sorrow they gave Aurelian a solemn burial, not far from the place where he had been killed. The Senate and the people of Rome were also in a state of disbelief and shock. In a solemn session of the Senate he was deified. With the death of

Aurelian, an emperor disappeared from the scene who had done everything to stop the decline of the Empire.

Scriptores Historiae Augustae, *Aurelianus* 36–37
Zosimus 1.62

TACITUS
c. 200–early July 276
Emperor from late 275

Everyone expected the armies to appoint a new emperor from their own ranks, but that did not happen. Perhaps the army was too shocked by Aurelian's death to take any action. Yet the Senate did not seem particularly eager to make a move either. Thus an interregnum was proclaimed while the Senate and the army searched for a suitable successor. Eventually they decided on Tacitus, a seventy-five-year-old senator. He was not a particularly appealing figure. A sober-minded man, he was almost never in the limelight and was not known to be someone who had his mind set on becoming emperor. When he was offered the throne he initially tried to dodge the responsibility, retiring to his estate near Baiae on the Gulf of Naples. But in the end he let himself be persuaded and entered Rome as emperor, almost two months after his predecessor had been murdered. He named his half-brother Florianus prefect of the imperial guard.

Tacitus remained in Rome for only a short time and soon left for the east to tackle the problems there. He trekked through Asia Minor, defeating the Goths, who had penetrated deep into the Empire. However, he avoided a confrontation with the Persians, who were still active on the eastern border, and planned on returning to Rome. He never arrived, dying on the homeward journey in early July 276, according to some in Tyana in Cappadocia, according to others in Tarsus or in Pontus. There are no details about his death, but it is generally assumed that he fell victim to a military plot. The plot was apparently connected to the assassination of the governor Maximinus, a close relative of Tacitus' who had been killed by a number of army officers. Maximinus had been appointed by the emperor himself and, afraid of being punished, the officers decided to get rid of the emperor. But it is also possible that Tacitus succumbed to disease. Colourless as he was, his name soon sank into oblivion. Perhaps the Senate's lack of interest contributed to that: he was not deified, but by the same token he was also spared the *damnatio memoriae*, the destruction of any traces of his reign.

Scriptores Historiae Augustae, *Tacitus* 13 and *Probus* 10
Aurelius Victor, *Liber de Caesaribus* 36
Zosimus 1.63

FLORIANUS
?–September 276
Emperor from July 276

Florianus, Tacitus' half-brother, yearned to be emperor and promptly claimed the throne. The Senate consented. There is no way of knowing whether this occurred spontaneously or under pressure from the ambitious Florianus. In the western provinces he was accepted as emperor, but in the east, in Egypt, Syria, Palestine and Phoenicia, there was a preference for another man, Probus, who was officially proclaimed emperor by the troops. One of the two would have to step aside. Probus took decisive action right away. At the head of his army he headed to Asia Minor to meet Florianus on the battlefield.

The two strongmen met near Tarsus, the capital of Cilicia. Florianus had more troops, but Probus' soldiers were better trained. They were from the eastern provinces and were more accustomed to the heat. Moreover Probus was known to be a shrewd tactician. This became clear in the weeks that both armies were encamped not far from each other. Florianus wanted to force a decision, whereas Probus, by contrast, tried to avoid a confrontation, hoping to bring his opponent's troops to their knees by exhausting them. And that was exactly what happened. The morale of Florianus' troops sank rapidly, and when soldiers who were partial to Probus began to sow discord among the ranks, the opposition quickly crumbled. Florianus tried to turn the tide, but the soldiers refused to listen to him any more. A short time later, in September, he was killed in Tarsus. He was emperor for a little longer than eighty-eight days and was the third emperor to be forced from power in less than a year.

Scriptores Historiae Augustae, *Tacitus* 14
Aurelius Victor, *Liber de Caesaribus* 37
Eutropius 9.16
Zosimus 1.64

PROBUS
19 August 232–late September 282
Emperor from the summer of 276

Probus was born in Sirmium, of humble origins. Like many other emperors of the third century he was a real career soldier, but – and this was less common – he was also popular with the Senate and people of Rome. He respected the old Roman traditions. This was evident just after the death of Florianus. Although at that moment he was already in power, he sent the Senate a letter, asking that he be invested with the imperial rank.

For the first two years of his reign he had his hands full fighting the Vandals, Franks and Burgundians on the Rhine and Danube borders and the Gothic tribes who were breaching the borders on the lower reaches of the Danube. It was apparently also during that time that he waged war on the Persians, because at the end of 279 he had taken the title Persicus. Just when he thought peace had been restored to the Empire and he could devote himself to improving government organisation and the infrastructure in Rome, he was confronted with a number of pretenders to the throne. In Cologne, Proculus and Bonosus proclaimed themselves emperor in 280. It is uncertain if they were acting together or as individuals. In any case Probus succeeded in vanquishing them, doing the same thing a year later with Saturninus, who had been proclaimed leader by the troops in Syria.

In late 281 Probus was in Rome to attend a great triumphal procession and to present gladiatorial matches, for which four thousand swordsmen and the most exotic animals from all over the Empire had been brought in. Around that time Aurelian's wall, which was supposed to protect Rome from invaders, was completed.

Yet even Probus did not escape a violent death. It was probably a speech that he gave to his soldiers, whom he was leading to the eastern border to wipe out the last remnants of the Persian threat, that proved to be his undoing. He apparently hinted at a period of peace in the Empire, when a strong army would no longer be an absolute necessity. But the soldiers, who looked forward to the plunder of war, did not take kindly to his words, and his popularity plummeted. When he started deploying them extensively for all sorts of projects, such as draining swamps, harvesting crops and improving harbour facilities, the soldiers began to hate him.

In September 282 things got out of hand. Probus had given the soldiers the task of draining a swamp in the vicinity of his birth-place Sirmium in preparation for the excavation of a canal to the river Save. A number of them revolted and attacked the emperor. Probus had to flee to a watch-tower inlaid with iron, which had been built to supervise the work. The soldiers followed him into the watch-tower and cut him down with their swords.

It is unclear if there was any direct link between Probus' murder and a revolt that had broken out at that moment among the armies of Raetia and Noricum. In any case the soldiers joined the rebels there and recognised Carus, the commander of the imperial guard, as the new emperor. Although the official propaganda did every-thing to eradicate the memory of Probus by striking his name from all inscriptions, he has nevertheless gone down as one of the best emperors of the third century.

Scriptores Historiae Augustae, Probus 20–21
Aurelius Victor, Liber de Caesaribus 37
Zosimus 1.71

CARUS
c. 224–July/August 283
Emperor from August/September 282

Carus, born in Narbonne, was a very different man from Probus. He did not ask the Senate to ratify his new position but simply gave them an ultimatum after being proclaimed emperor in September. He gave his two sons Carinus and Numerian the title Caesar, as well as a number of official responsibilities. While Carinus stayed behind in Rome to supervise the situation in the west, he and Numerian left for the east. After first prosecuting a successful war against the Sarmatians on the Danube, he then turned his attention to the east and the Persians. Infighting had seriously weakened their position, and Carus saw a chance to end the war that had been begun by Aurelian and Probus once and for all.

Carus had penetrated deep into Mesopotamia and made camp not far from Ctesiphon, when he suddenly died, at the very moment that total victory was within his grasp. The sources do not offer any definitive answer as to what happened on that day in July or August 283. The only thing that is certain is that a storm broke out that was so violent that everything grew black and no one could see past the end of his nose. Lightning bolts and thunder claps made the whole thing even more terrifying. Suddenly the air was filled with cries that the emperor was dead. Had he been struck by lightning while he lay sick in bed, or had someone taken advantage of the darkness to kill him? If the latter, it might have been the prefect of the imperial guard Aper, the father-in-law of Carus' son Numerian, who wanted to clear the way for his son-in-law, but this is nothing more than speculation. Carus was only in power for six months.

Scriptores Historiae Augustae, *Carus* 8
Aurelius Victor, *Liber de Caesaribus* 38
Eutropius 9.18

NUMERIAN
c. 253–November 284
Emperor from July/August 283

Carus' two sons were now in charge, Carinus in the west and Numerian in the east. Numerian was the better natured of the two, but seemed less suited for the task at hand. He was more interested in the fine arts and rhetoric than in matters of state. This meant that his father-in-law Aper was able to exert a powerful influence over him. It was also Aper's decision to suspend the campaign against the Persians and pull the troops out of Mesopotamia.

Much of what happened during the difficult retreat must have escaped Numerian' attention because his eyesight was severely limited as a result of an ocular disease. To protect his eyes from the bright light he was taken from place to place in a coach that was kept dark by curtains. In November 284, in the vicinity of Nicomedia, Aper felt that the moment had come to seize power and he had the nearly blind Numerian killed. But he could not keep the truth a secret because the soldiers sensed that something was amiss and began inquiring about the absent emperor. Aper first claimed that because of his eye condition Numerian could not bear the daylight and the strong wind, which caused the sand to blow around. But after the men started to notice a terrible stench, he could no longer keep the emperor's death a secret. The soldiers grabbed hold of him and dragged him away. At a mass gathering of the army Aper was found guilty of murder and sentenced to death. The sentence was carried out by the man the soldiers immediately proclaimed emperor: Diocles. He pointed his sword at the sun, swore an oath that he had had nothing to do with Numerian's death – there were rumours that he and Aper had been in league with each other – and cut down Aper in front of the assembled soldiers.

Scriptores Historiae Augustae, *Numerianus* 14
Aurelius Victor, *Liber de Caesaribus* 38
Eutropius 9.18

CARINUS
c. 250–August/September 285
Emperor from the spring of 283

Once again there were two emperors: in the east, Diocles, who would soon change his name to Diocletian, and Numerian's brother Carinus in the west. A clash between them was inevitable. The two men were complete opposites: the forthright Diocletian, born into a simple peasant family in Pannonia, tremendously strong, good-looking and every inch a soldier, and the spoiled, malicious and perverse Carinus. It was whispered that Carinus' conduct was reminiscent of Commodus' and Heliogabalus' and that his private life was one licentious adventure after the next. He took pleasure in seducing as many men and women as possible. He was supposedly married more than nine times, impregnating most of his wives and then sending them away. Those who dared to criticise him were risking their lives to do so. His reign was reportedly characterised by great luxury. Lavish parties were the order of the day. None of that altered the fact that he took his government tasks seriously. In 285 he dealt with a certain Julianus, who had had himself proclaimed emperor in northern Italy. Carinus seemed to be in control of the situation.

But the threat posed by Diocletian was of a different magnitude. Supported by the governor of Dalmatia, Constantius, who made sure that the Danube armies did not side with Carinus, Diocletian made rapid progress in his march to the west. But in spite of this misfortune Carinus raised a vast army, much larger than Diocletian's. In the spring of 285 the two armies faced each other, near the Margus (Morava), not far from Belgrade. At first it looked as if Carinus would win the day. The lines of Diocletian's army were forced to retreat and a breakthrough seemed to be a matter of hours. But suddenly their progress faltered. Confusion took hold of Carinus' soldiers, and Diocletian's army fought its way back. It soon became clear why Carinus' army had lost its will to fight: Carinus had been killed, not by the enemy, but by one of his own officers, whose wife he had once seduced. His soldiers saw no reason to go on fighting and swore an oath of allegiance to Diocletian, who was now the undisputed ruler of the Roman Empire. Any reminder of Carus, Numerian and Carinus was destroyed. Their memory was damned.

Scriptores Historiae Augustae, *Carinus* 18
Aurelius Victor, *Liber de Caesaribus* 39
Zosimus 1.73

7

DIOCLETIAN AND
THE TETRARCHY

Diocletian's coup marked the start of a new period in Roman history. He put an end to the anarchy that had paralysed the Empire economically and politically for so long and laid the foundations for a new form of government, in which the role of the Senate was greatly restricted.

Diocletian was a man of action who had grown up in the army. Perhaps that was why it was so clear to him that discipline in the military had broken down and a restoration of that discipline was a prerequisite for restoring order to the Empire. In addition to that, almost immediately after his accession he saw to it that the armies were made more mobile. In the interior, within the borders, he stationed the so-called *comitatenses*, soldiers on horseback who could reach threatened areas quickly.

In the long term he focused his attention on the organisation of the Empire. In his view it had grown too large and too complex to be governed by one man. We should not discount the possibility that it was a coup led by Carausius, the commander of the Roman fleet in Britain, that made him realise that only shared responsibility could neutralise the danger of insurrections. For six years, from 287 to 293, Carausius ruled Britain. Then he was murdered by one of his subordinates, Allectus, who was only removed from power and killed in 297. To counteract such takeovers Diocletian designed a system of government, the tetrarchy, in which he himself was in charge but in which a share of the leadership was delegated to a co-emperor (Augustus) and two sub-emperors (Caesares), who in time would become the new emperors and appoint two new sub-emperors of their own.

In 293 the system was complete. Diocletian and his co-emperor Maximian were the highest-ranking officials. Diocletian reigned in the east, with Galerius as his sub-emperor, Maximian controlled the west with Constantius as adjutant. All four claimed the right to be worshipped as gods. Diocletian named himself after the supreme god of the Romans, Jupiter Jovius, while Maximian identified with Hercules. Binding the tetrarchs together was their Illyrian military background. Marriages were supposed to cement those ties. Valeria, Diocletian's daughter, was married off to Galerius, and Constantius married Theodora, Maximian's daughter (or step-daughter). That might be the reason why the system worked so well in the beginning and why the Senate saw no chance to play the four rulers off against one another. The new division of power meant an infringement on the position of Rome. It remained the nominal capital of the Empire, but the real power lay in the cities of Nicomedia, Milan, Sirmium and Trier. The Senate played no role in either the selection of emperors or the governance of the Empire. Diocletian accepted counsel only from a group of personal advisers who sat on a special committee, the *consortium sacrum*. The distance between the emperor and his subjects widened. If the emperors of the first and second centuries had functioned as *princeps*, the first of the Senate and the nation, this changed completely under Diocletian. He could be approached only by means of court protocol. Like an Oriental king he dressed in a purple cloak and wore a diadem on his head. He considered himself the *dominus*, the lord of his subjects. His form of imperial rule became known as the Dominate.

Maintaining the armies, waging successful military campaigns in many parts of the Empire, supporting the immense bureaucracy and the imperial courts of Diocletian and his fellow monarchs – all these things cost money. Because the traditional tax system was not generating sufficient revenue – the measures taken in order to bring better money into circulation and thereby stabilise prices did not have the desired effect – the emperors instituted a system in which a special tax was levied on various subsections of the population on the basis of land ownership. It became impossible to move into another group with fewer obligations. Occupations were made hereditary. Officials of the city government, artisans and peasants, everyone was bound to his profession. Social mobility was reduced to nil. Even prices were fixed from the top down.

Shortly after 300, Diocletian and Galerius initiated a large-scale programme of anti-Christian persecutions. In their pursuit of religious unity they wanted to eradicate the Christians, whose numbers were on the rise. On 24 February 303 an edict was issued that paved the way for the burning of Christian texts and the destruction of Christian churches. More such edicts were to follow. More than ever before, Christians were faced with a choice: perform a sacrifice to the emperor or be killed.

CONSTANTIUS I
31 March 250–25 July 306
(Sub-)emperor from 1 March 293

In 305 Diocletian felt that he had been in power long enough and there were ample safeguards to keep the new form of government in place. And so he stepped down. But at that point it became clear how hard it can be for rulers to relinquish power voluntarily. It was only through Diocletian's pressure that Maximian was prepared to resign from office. On 1 May their abdication was solemnly confirmed in a double ceremony in Milan and Nicomedia. Constantius and Galerius became the new emperors, Maximinus Daia and Severus the sub-emperors. But in contrast to Diocletian, who was reportedly not in the best of health, Maximian had trouble adjusting to the life of a private citizen. In fact he only managed to stay away from the business of government for a year.

The situation changed drastically with the death of the first tetrarch, Constantius, on 25 July 306 in York. He wanted to cross to Britain from Boulogne in order to halt the advance of the Scots and the Picts, who had invaded from the north. Although he had been in poor health for some time, there was no indication that he was at death's door. But then the symptoms started appearing of a serious disease – it is unknown exactly which one – and his condition quickly deteriorated. According to the writer Lactantius, he sent a letter to Maximian with the request that he allow his son Constantine, who was staying with Maximian because he had a relationship with the latter's daughter Fausta, to come to him. Probably sensing what was going to happen, Maximian did everything he could to stop Constantine, but he managed to escape anyway. Making use of the horses of the Roman postal service, he raced over the imperial roads to the Channel coast and crossed to Britain with his father. Because his father was in no position to lead the troops, Constantine took his place and defeated the Scots and the Picts. When he returned to the encampment at York he saw that his father was dying. In his last will Constantius transferred command of the troops to him and invested him with the imperial rank. After doing so, he breathed his last. The soldiers mourned the loss of their beloved emperor, but were elated that he had decided to appoint Constantine as his successor. The end of the tetrarchy was already in sight

Eutropius 10.1–2
Aurelius Victor, *Liber de Caesaribus* 40
Lactantius, *On the Death of the Persecutors* 24

SEVERUS
?–16 September 307
(Sub-)emperor from 1 May 305

On 28 October 306 the Senate and the imperial guard proclaimed Maximian's son Maxentius emperor. Emperor Galerius sent his sub-emperor Severus to bring him into line. To give his position some semblance of legitimacy Maxentius invited his father to be his co-emperor. The latter was not averse to the idea, but he first wrote a letter to Diocletian, in which he explained to him how critical the situation in the Empire had become and that the circumstances called for swift action. Without waiting for a reply, he left Campania or Lucania, where he had been spending his retirement following his abdication, and hurried to his son's side. When he arrived, the danger had already receded. Severus, who had been promoted to emperor by Galerius, proved to be no match for Maxentius. His soldiers deserted him and defected to the other side. He fled to Ravenna, where he surrendered to Maximian after the latter's solemn pledge that his life would be spared. But despite that he was brought to Rome and presented to the populace as an object of scorn and ridicule. In Tres Tabernae, a small town on the Via Appia sixty kilometres from Rome, he was imprisoned and executed. That was on 16 September 307. Some accounts claim that he was forced to commit suicide by opening his veins.

Lactantius, *On the Death of the Persecutors* 26
Aurelius Victor, *Liber de Caesaribus* 40.7
Anonymus Valesianus 4.10
Zosimus 2.10

MAXIMIAN
21 July 250–July 310
Emperor from October/December 285 to 1 May 305

Maximian died three years later, in July 310. Diocletian's personal intercession at a conference in Carnuntum in 308 prevented him from becoming emperor again. It seemed as if his ambitions had been curbed, but the opposite was true. He retired to the residence of his son-in-law Constantine in Gaul, but scheming seemed to be in his blood. Although Constantine treated him with the greatest respect, what he really wanted was to return to the throne. In July 310 he saw his chance. Constantine was embroiled in a war with rebellious Gauls, and Maximian made use of his absence to proclaim himself emperor. However, Constantine soon made it clear that he was not to be trifled with. He immediately took military action against his father-in-law, who had taken cover in the city of Arles. But before he was able to mount a defence of the city, Constantine was already at the gates. Maximian fled to Marseilles, where he was captured by Constantine.

The sources are vague and one-sided in their description of the confrontation in Marseilles between father-in-law and son-in-law. Lactantius and Eusebius provide us with the most detailed accounts. They paint a picture of a merciful Constantine, who forgave Maximian his misdeeds and spared his life. Maximian is the complete antithesis of that. He is portrayed as a man who was so perverted by his lust for power and so incensed about the humiliation to which he had been subjected that he showed no gratitude whatsoever, responding with fresh attempts to eliminate Constantine. For this he enlisted the help of his daughter Fausta, Constantine's wife. He promised her a different husband, someone who would be a better match for her. But she took Constantine's side and informed him of her father's plan. Constantine immediately took precautions. After nightfall he had a eunuch take his place in his bedroom – presumably in bed – while he himself hid nearby. Maximian entered the dark room and killed the eunuch. He ran outside, in high spirits because he was convinced that he had killed Constantine. At that moment Constantine appeared with a group of soldiers. Maximian was arrested and placed in custody. A magnanimous Constantine supposedly forgave him. Shortly thereafter, however, in late July 310, Maximian was found hanging from a rope in one of the rooms in the palace. We will never know whether he took his own life or was put to death by the man he had wanted to kill. One thing we can be sure about is that with his death, the most untrustworthy of the tetrarchs exited the political stage.

Lactantius, *On the Death of the Persecutors* 30
Eusebius, *Life of Constantine* 1.47
Eutropius 10.3
Zosimus 2.11

GALERIUS
c. 260–May 311
Emperor from 21 May 293

Almost a year later, in May 311, Galerius died. He had been a hard man, ruthless towards anyone who crossed his path, particularly Christians. Together with his sub-emperor Maximinus Daia, he organised mass persecutions. According to the Christian writers Lactantius and Eusebius, his final days were completely consistent with his awful reign. With undisguised delight they describe how he was visited by God's vengeance. It was Galerius' just deserts for everything he had done to the Christians. In 310 the symptoms appeared of a festering testicular infection, which grew into an enormous tumour, probably the result of testicular cancer. With a great sense for the sensational, Lactantius writes that worms devoured him from the inside out and he literally rotted away, wracked by agonising pain. The doctors were powerless to help. Some of them could not bear the stench and turned away, retching; this infuriated the emperor and cost the physicians their heads. In the end Galerius' body was nothing but a formless lump. His upper body was completely desiccated and his thin skin clung to his ribcage. His lower body fell like a pudding and his feet lost their shape.

His suffering went on for a year. According to the Christian writers, in May 311, when Galerius knew that he did not have much longer to live, he supposedly exclaimed that God truly lived.

He then reportedly stopped all persecutions of the Christians and converted to Christianity on his deathbed. A few days later he died.

Lactantius, *On the Death of the Persecutors* 33–34
Eusebius, *Ecclesiastical History* 8.16
Zosimus 2.11
Anonymus Valesianus 3.8

DIOCLETIAN
22 December 245–3 December 311 (or later)
Emperor from 20 November 284 to 1 May 305

Not much later the founder of the tetrarchy, Diocletian, also passed away. Following his abdication he retired to his palace in Spalatum (Split) on the Croatian coast. It is hard to say if he was happy there, because he consistently maintained his seclusion and few reports ever came out about his personal life. The only time he broke his isolation was in 308, during the conference in Carnuntum. What he did in seclusion in the years that followed is lost to history. According to the pagan authors he spent his days growing vegetables and, reasonably satisfied with what he accomplished, he died a peaceful death. Christian writers on the other hand suggest that his later years were very unhappy and culminated in a sad demise. By their accounts the rise of Constantine and the dissolution of the tetrarchy were more than Diocletian could bear, and he slowly sank into madness. Plagued by fearsome visions he decided to end his life. But the man who had once made the most difficult decisions with the greatest of ease was now at a loss how to take his own life. He roamed the palace halls, screaming and crying as a result of the madness that had taken hold of his mind. He refused all food and drink. Writhing in pain and tormented by delusions he eventually succeeded in starving himself to death. According to Lactantius this was God's revenge for everything Diocletian had done to the Christians. The date of his death is unknown. The date most often reported is December 311, but it is also possible that he died in 312 or 313.

Eutropius 9.28
Lactantius, *On the Death of the Persecutors* 42
Zosimus 2.7

8

CONSTANTINE AND THE STRUGGLE FOR POWER

During Diocletian's final years it had become clear that the tetrarchy had in fact become unworkable because the leading players – Constantine, Maxentius, Licinius and Maximinus Daia – mainly looked after their own interests. They kept a close eye on one another. The first two operated in the west, the other two in the east.

MAXENTIUS
c. 275/278 or 283–28 October 312
Emperor from 28 October 306

The first to drop out of the picture was Maxentius. Their relationship having hit an all-time low, Constantine decided to get rid of his brother-in-law. In the summer of 312 he left Gaul and began the march to Italy. One city after another fell into his hands, and in mid-October he reached the walls of Rome. Maxentius got scared; he feared treason, since the people and the Senate had a tendency to side with the enemy. He consulted the Sibylline books and read that on 28 October an enemy of Rome would die. This gave him confidence and he decided to fight Constantine that day. The armies of Maxentius and Constantine met at the Milvian Bridge over the Tiber, a few kilometres north of the city walls of Rome.

It would become one of the most famous battles in Roman history, but that is mainly because of Constantine's pronouncement after the battle that he owed his victory to the God of the Christians. There are two versions of God's supposed involvement. They differ from each other on several essential points. According to Lactantius, the night before the battle Constantine dreamed that he was ordered to put the sign of Christ on the soldiers' shields. It is assumed that this was the chi-rho symbol, the first two letters of the Greek form of 'Christ' in a monogram. Constantine did what was asked of him and won the battle. From that moment on he believed in the power of the Christian God.

Twenty-five years later Eusebius offered a different version. In his *Life of Constantine* he writes that Constantine had told him under oath how it had all come about; frightened by the evil practices and magic arts of his rival, he had sought Christ's help. Around noon on the day before the battle he supposedly saw a cross of light in the sky and the words *Hoc signo victor eris* ('By this sign you will be victorious'). That night Christ appeared to him and instructed him to put the heavenly symbol on the army standards. He apparently did so, with the desired result.

It is hard to reconcile the two versions with each other. Lactantius' version is the more credible. To be sure Eusebius' account goes into greater depth, but it is suspect, mainly because it is never really clear what exactly Constantine saw: the sign of the cross, a sign resembling a cross or the monogram of Christ. The only thing that seems certain is that Constantine had an experience that he, or the advisers he consulted, interpreted as the power of the God of the Christians and that this experience moved him to convert to Christianity.

The authors have far less to say about the battle itself. Maxentius had left the city in the firm belief that he would win the day. He had positioned his troops on a plain, with the Tiber behind them. In the course of the battle he realised that Constantine's army was much stronger. His horsemen were being crushed by Constantine's cavalry, and his infantry was retreating under the pressure of the enemy's shock troops. For a time his men were able to stand their ground, but they were too badly outnumbered. Their only option was flight. In utter disarray they ran towards the Tiber. Many were trampled. They were left with broken limbs on the battlefield, where they were slaughtered by the enemy. The survivors had pinned their hopes to a bateau bridge that Maxentius had had built specifically as an escape route. The plan was to destroy the bridge as soon as their pursuers were on it. But the plan backfired. The bridge could not hold the weight of the fleeing masses and gave way. Maxentius' soldiers ended up in the water and drowned. Only a handful made it to the other side. Maxentius, who was on horseback, reached the bridge after it had collapsed and was driven into the river by enemy soldiers. He tried to reach the other side by swimming there with his horse, but he was caught up in the current and drowned. For Eusebius, the outcome of the battle was no surprise: it was perfectly obvious that God had sided with Constantine and had punished Maxentius for his godless deeds, in the same way that He had once punished Pharaoh and the Egyptians when they tried to prevent Moses and the Jews from leaving Egypt.

Lactantius, *The Death of the Persecutors* 40–44
Eusebius, *Life of Constantine* 1.38
Ecclesiastical History 9.9
Zosimus 2.16

MAXIMINUS DAIA
20 November 270 or 285–August 313
(Sub-)emperor from 1 May 305

Constantine was now the undisputed ruler of the west. In the east there were still two rivals: Licinius and Maximinus Daia. With both men aspiring to absolute power, the situation became increasingly tense. A war between the two was only a matter of time. Constantine hoped that Licinius would come out the winner, since his half-sister Constantia had married Licinius in Milan in February 313, and at that occasion both emperors had agreed to pursue a common religious policy. Seven months later those agreements were officially set down in the Edict of Milan. The persecution of Christians seemed to be a thing of the past.

During Licinius' stay in Milan, Maximinus Daia swung into action after being proclaimed emperor by his troops. He left Syria and headed west, passed Bithynia, crossed the Bosporus and conquered Byzantium and Heraclea, cities which until then had been in the hands of Licinius' supporters. Licinius headed out to meet his enemy on the battlefield, even though at that moment his force numbered no more than thirty thousand soldiers, while Maximinus Daia had over seventy thousand. On 30 April the decisive confrontation took place, not far from Adrianopolis in Thrace, and Licinius emerged victorious.

The events that followed were placed by Lactantius as well as Eusebius in a highly Christian context. Both writers make it seem as if God himself had intervened once again, just as He did a year before in Rome at the Milvian Bridge. Maximinus fled the battlefield in a cloak that he had taken from a slave. He hoped to discourage his rival from pursuit by building forts at the passes of the Taurus Mountains, but this proved to be a vain hope. Licinius was not to be stopped and advanced on Tarsus, where Maximinus' forces were entrenched.

There, so writes Lactantius, in the summer of 313 the beleaguered Maximinus saw no other way out of the misfortunes God had visited upon him but death. He chose poison, but before he took it he sat down to an extravagant last meal with lots of wine. This had the effect that the highly toxic and normally fast-acting poison was not completely absorbed by his overly full stomach and death was slow in coming. In the interim he went completely mad. Tormented by stabbing pains in his stomach and abdomen he even began to eat dirt. His death throes went on for four days. Eventually the pain became more than he could bear. He slammed his head into a wall and his eyes literally fell out of their sockets. At that moment the blind Maximinus supposedly saw God and confessed on his deathbed that Christ was the true God.

Lactantius, On the Death of the Persecutors 49
Eusebius, The Life of Constantine 1.58–59
Aurelius Victor, Liber de Caesaribus 41
Zosimus 2.17

LICINIUS
c. 265–spring 325
(Sub-)emperor from 11 November 308 to
10 September 324

Constantine and Licinius were too ambitious and too fixated on their own glory and success for any sort of partnership to last long. The Christian writers place the blame for the rift squarely on Licinius' shoulders, but this is a misrepresentation of reality. Constantine certainly also had his part in the split, which became apparent around 315. He rejected Licinius' request to appoint his son Licinius, whose mother was Constantine's half-sister Constantia, as sub-emperor and chose another candidate himself: Bassianus, the husband of another half-sister, Anastasia. Licinius took exception to this. After a number of military confrontations a compromise was reached in 317: Constantine's sons Crispus and Constantine and Licinius' son

Licinius were appointed sub-emperors. Few if any really believed that this solution would be of a lasting character, all the more so since Constantine was mainly making overtures to the Christians, whose number was growing rapidly, while Licinius was supported primarily by pagan intellectuals. He barred Christians from holding public office, though that policy did not lead to large-scale persecutions.

The definitive war between the two broke out in 321. Constantine drove the Sarmatians back across the Danube and wanted to do the same with the Goths, who were wreaking havoc in Thrace. Licinius regarded this as an intrusion on his policy in the east and complained that Constantine had violated the agreements they had made. A military confrontation was inevitable. On 3 July 324 they faced each other on the battlefield, near Adrianopolis. Constantine was the victor and Licinius fled, first to Byzantium and then, when the ground started getting too hot under his feet there, to Chalcedon in Bithynia. He left behind the commander of his personal bodyguard Martinianus to halt Constantine's advance. In the meantime he hoped to raise an army and defeat Constantine. But that plan failed, and he suffered his second defeat that year at Chrysopolis on 18 September.

Licinius' wife Constantia hurried to her half-brother's headquarters at once to plead for her husband's life. Constantine received her, talked with her and promised to spare Licinius' life, after which the latter surrendered in good faith. He was given permission to settle in Thessaloniki as a private citizen. But a few months later, in the spring of 325, Constantine suddenly gave the order to hang Licinius. Why he changed his mind and had Licinius executed is a mystery. Eusebius says that the punishment was Licinius' come-uppance for his past misdeeds and leaves the matter at that. Zosimus and Eutropius have a different opinion, but their accounts are just as superficial as Eusebius', and they confine themselves to the observation that with this decision Constantine had violated a solemn oath. In the next century the explanation was dreamt up that Licinius had sought contact with Germanic tribes on the Danube in order to stage a coup.

Eusebius, *Life of Constantine* 2.58–59
Zosimus 2.28
Anonymus Valesianus 5.29
Eutropius 10.5

CONSTANTINE I
27 February 272/273–22 May 337
Emperor from 25 July 306

Constantine I was now the sole sovereign and could devote himself to realising his plans. He increasingly took on the role of champion of the Christian cause. He saw himself as a monarch who had been sent by God, a ruler who was not only responsible for the welfare of the state, but also had a duty to ensure the unity of the Christians. He considered himself to be both a temporal and a spiritual leader, 'leader by the grace of God', and God's representative on earth. In that capacity he could claim a leading role in theological discussions, as was the case during the Council of Nicea in 324, where the divinity of Christ and the relationship between God the Father, God the Son and the Holy Spirit was debated. Arius, a priest from Alexandria, took the position that there was a hierarchy within the Godhead, with the Father as 'the' God and the Son as his inferior. The council of three hundred bishops, which had been convened by Constantine I, condemned Arius' denial of the divine nature of the Son as heresy.

Constantine I now made no secret of his policy of Christianisation. Christians were given priority when it came to filling official positions, and pagan functionaries were forbidden from performing sacrifices to their gods. In pastoral letters bishops announced the construction of state-funded churches. The Christians in Rome who lacked churches with sufficient space for their gatherings were given a number of large basilicas by Constantine I, the best known among them being Saint John Lateran's, the old Saint Peter's, the Holy Cross of Jerusalem, Saint Agnes Outside the Walls and Saint Sebastian's. Monumental churches were built on sacred places in the Holy Land: in Bethlehem, the Church of the Nativity and in Jerusalem, the Church of the Holy Sepulchre.

The preferential treatment went even further. Christian communities in various cities, principally Rome, were the recipients of enormous rural estates and palaces. At least as important in the long run was the fact that all donations and bequests received by the Church were exempt from taxation. In this way Church holdings grew at a rapid tempo, and in time the Church became the largest landowner after the emperor.

One of the high points of Constantine's reign was the solemn dedication of a new city, Constantinople (city of Constantine), on the site of the old Byzantium, on 11 May 330. Constantine regarded this city as the new Rome, a copy of the old Rome. Like its predecessor this city stood on seven hills, consisted of fourteen districts and a forum and its own Senate. Constantinople was the clear proof that the centre of gravity of the Empire had shifted to the east.

A low point in Constantine's reign is the murder of his son Crispus, a child from his first marriage, with Minervina. Crispus had been appointed sub-emperor in 317. In March 326 he was killed, for reasons that have never come to light. One version of the story is that Constantine's then-wife Fausta was having a relationship with him and when Crispus broke it off she accused him of adultery in front of Constantine, knowing full well that the emperor had recently issued a law criminalising adultery. But it is also possible that Fausta insisted on Crispus' execution in order to clear the way for her own sons. Fausta herself would also meet an unhappy end. Helena, Constantine's mother, succeeded in convincing her son that Crispus had been falsely accused. Fausta withdrew to the bathroom, filled the bathtub with boiling hot water and died.

Constantine I himself died on 22 May 337, on Pentecost, after becoming seriously ill two months earlier, just before Easter. The nature of his illness is not known. He tried to find treatment in Drepanum and had prayed at the grave of the martyr Lucianus, one of the favourite saints of his mother, Helena. He then left for Nicomedia, where he convened a solemn gathering of bishops. He explained to them that he had always wanted to be baptised in the Jordan – despite reports to the contrary, he had never been baptised – but that in view of his illness it was too late for that now. The honour of baptising Constantine fell to Eusebius, bishop of Nicomedia (not to be confused with Eusebius the bishop-writer from Caesarea). Not everyone was happy with this choice, as there were stories that Eusebius was a follower of the ideas of Arius.

CONSTANTINE AND THE STRUGGLE FOR POWER

In the last weeks of his life Constantine no longer wore the imperial purple and the diadem, but went about in the white garment of the 'newborn'. Fully prepared for death, he passed away in one of his villas in Nicomedia. His personal bodyguard placed his body in a golden coffin draped with a pall of imperial purple before it was taken to Constantinople. He lay there in state, first in the imperial palace and later in the Church of the Holy Apostles, which Constantine had had built for himself. In the church there were twelve sarcophagi bearing the names of the apostles. By placing his sarcophagus next to the others, he was symbolically made the thirteenth apostle.

When the news of his death and burial became known in Rome, the nation reacted with dismay, angry that the Emperor of Rome had preferred to be buried in Constantinople. The Senate was less consistent and in accordance with old tradition declared Constantine a god. The first Christian emperor deified: the Roman Empire had definitely changed.

Eusebius, *Life of Constantine* 4.62–67
Zosimus 2.39

9

THE DYNASTY OF CONSTANTINE

If Constantine can be blamed for anything, it is his failure to make any clear arrangements for his succession. From a man who had orchestrated so much, you would have expected better. Maybe he had put off the decision because he knew how great the rivalry was among his three sons and realised that none of the three would accept one of the others being put forward as absolute ruler. As a consequence of Constantine's negligence the throne was empty for nearly three months. Then the army in Constantinople took action, expressing its preference for a tripartite government of all three sons. Other pretenders to the throne, such as Constantine's nephews Hannibalianus and Dalmatius, were disposed of. Only a few members of his family escaped death. Of them, Julian and Gallus, both of whom would later play a prominent role, are the best known.

CONSTANTINE II
7 August 316–early April 340
Emperor from 9 September 337

In early September 337, Constantine's sons were proclaimed emperors by the army in Pannonia. Constantine II would rule Gaul, Britain and Spain; Constantius II would be given control over the east; and Constans would get Italy, Africa and Illyria.

This arrangement lasted less than three years. As the oldest of the three sons, Constantine enjoyed the greatest respect. He also acted as regent for Constans, who as a teenager was considered too young to be able to discharge all his duties on his own. In the spring of 340 the issue of who would control Italy led to an open rift between the two brothers. Constantine took his supervisory role quite literally and began to eye up Constans' territory. He raised an army to put his brother in his place. In the spring of 340 he left Gaul, crossed the Alps and invaded northern Italy. But the outcome was not the one he had envisioned. Constans, at that moment in Moesia, sent troops to the threatened area. Near Aquileia they set up an ambush for Constantine. He was killed, as was a large part of his army. His body was thrown into the river Alsa.

Zosimus 2.41
Aurelius Victor, *Liber de Caesaribus* 42.21

CONSTANS
320/323–18 January 350
Emperor from 9 September 337

The death of Constantine simplified the situation in so far as Constans now added his older brother's territory to his own and ruled over the west, while Constantius II reigned in the east. Though there was friction between the two emperors, particularly in matters of religion – Constans was a fierce opponent of Arianism, which Constantius, by contrast, embraced – tensions never escalated to the point of armed conflict. Constans ruled the west for another ten years, and his reign grew steadily worse as time wore on. He bled the populace dry with high taxes and sold public offices to the highest bidders. His popularity plummeted. Danger lurked even within his immediate circle.

A coup of former supporters cost him his head. The initiative was taken by Magnentius, a Frank by birth, who had already served under Constans' father. He was assured of the support of other ex-servicemen. On 18 January he proclaimed himself emperor in Autun, in northern France. While Constans was enjoying himself during a hunting party, the conspirators were at a festive get-together to celebrate the birthday of the son of Marcellinus, Magnentius' most loyal ally. At a certain moment Magnentius left the party, but he returned shortly thereafter, dressed in imperial purple. The revellers immediately proclaimed him emperor. This acclamation soon became public knowledge. Everyone, civilian and soldier alike, cheered for Magnentius. Before Constans was able to mount a defence the rebellion had spread across the whole of Gaul. His only choice was a shameful retreat. He fled south, abandoned by everyone. Only one officer, his blond lover, the Frank Laniogaisus, remained loyal to him. Constans was tracked down by an army unit under the command of Gaeso, one of Magnentius' generals, in a small town at the foot of the Pyrenees, which was named after his grandmother Helena Elne, located near what is now Le Perthus. He had just fled into a church and hoped he would be safe there. But his pursuers knew no mercy, dragging him outside and turning him over to Gaeso. We will never know whether he was strangled by Gaeso or forced to commit suicide.

Eutropius 10.9.4
Ammianus Marcellinus 15.5.16
Zosimus 2.42
John of Antioch, Fragment 172

VETRANIO
Before 290–after 350, probably 356
Emperor from 1 March 350–25 December 350

MAGNENTIUS
c. 303–10 August 353
Emperor from 18 January 350

Initially it seemed that Magnentius had the situation under control. Italy, Gaul, Africa and Spain were soon in his hands. But his attempts to gain control of the Danube lands and thus lay claim to all the territory that had formerly belonged to Constans foundered because of the actions of the armies in Pannonia. They proclaimed Vetranio, an elderly general, emperor. What compelled Vetranio to accept the offer is unknown. It is possible that he genuinely had imperial ambitions, but we should not rule out the possibility that he carried out his coup with the help of Constantius in order to form a buffer against Magnentius. In any case Constantius sent Vetranio an imperial diadem.

However, Vetranio was not a strong personality and did not quite know how to handle his newly acquired rank. For a time he leaned towards siding with Magnentius after all, but when Constantius appeared in the Balkans, he quickly back-pedalled. On 25 December 350 he met Constantius in the vicinity of Naissus. In front of the assembled troops, they both stepped on to a platform. Constantius began to speak. No one knows exactly what he said, but the end result was that old Vetranio was stripped of his imperial medals. Sobbing, he threw himself at Constantius' feet. The latter helped him up, took him by the hand and led him off the stage. During a dinner Constantius promised Vetranio an allowance so that he would be able to enjoy his retirement in peace. That would be another six pleasant years.

Now there was just one thing Constantius had on his mind: the 'holy war' against Magnentius, the murderer of his brother Constans. On 15 March 351 he appointed his cousin Gallus, who had escaped the purges, sub-emperor. Magnentius in turn named Decentius. In the late summer of 351 the rivals met at Mursa, near the confluence of the Drage and the Danube. It was a bloody confrontation, with Magnentius losing two-thirds of his troops and Constantius almost half of his. Magnentius narrowly managed to escape, entering Gaul via the Italian Alps. His position was clearly weakened, though he still managed to check the ambitions of a few pretenders to the throne. With a great deal of effort he managed to retain power in Gaul, but in the summer of 353 he had to abandon the Alpine passes that gave access to Gaul. In the battle of Mons Seleucus (La-Batie-Mont-Saléon) that followed he met with a crushing defeat and fled to Lyon. His soldiers saw no point in continuing the fight and only wanted to save their skins by turning Magnentius over to Constantius. They found the house where he was staying, surrounded it and placed him under house arrest. Magnentius realised that the game was up and there were only two options: an execution or suicide. He chose the latter, and first killed his mother, friends and family members before falling on his sword. His body was taken to Constantius, who had Magnentius' head chopped off and paraded it triumphantly around the army camp on a pole as persuasive evidence that he was now the sole, undisputed emperor. Magnentius' sub-emperor Decentius hanged himself eight days later.

Eutropius 10.11–12
Aurelius Victor, *Liber de Caesaribus* 42
Zosimus 2.44, 2.53
John of Antioch, Fragment 174
Zonaras 6.13.9

CONSTANTIUS II
7 August 317–3 November 361
Emperor from 9 September 337

While Constantius was sorting things out in the west, not everything was going smoothly in the east, and it was Gallus, the sub-emperor who had been appointed two years before, who was to blame. As a military man he possessed undeniable talent, in view of his success on the eastern border against the Persians. But his headstrong manner of policy-making made Constantius afraid of him. In 354 he sent an envoy to the east with the request that Gallus come to Italy. But because this envoy, Domitianus, had sought contact with his political opponents, Gallus ignored the order and killed the envoy. This caused tensions to escalate and made Constantius decide to dispose of Gallus. Was Gallus unaware of this, or did he think he could clear up the misunderstanding? Either way, in the end he acceded to the emperor's request to come to Italy. In October 354 he was arrested on the island Flamona near the city of Pola in Istria, subjected to an interrogation and, a few weeks later, sentenced to death. The execution was grisly. Like a common thief his hands were bound behind his back and his head was chopped off. His face was mutilated beyond recognition and his torso was left on the street as a formless lump.

In Gaul the situation after Magnentius' death was far from stable. In 355 a general, Silvanus, had attempted to become emperor, but he was murdered by his own troops. As a deterrent to other usurpers, Constantius appointed Julian, Gallus' half-brother, Caesar of the west on 6 November 355. Julian won a number of victories against

THE DYNASTY OF CONSTANTINE

the Franks and the Alamanni and made himself popular with the people by easing the tax burden. Constantius also had his share of success, particularly on the Danube border, but he did not have much time to enjoy it because the aggressive Persians on the eastern border demanded his full attention. In Constantinople in the autumn of 359 the emperor readied himself for a military campaign. He asked Julian to part with a portion of his troops, but the soldiers revolted in February 360 and proclaimed Julian emperor. For the second time Constantius' position was being undermined from the west. The emperor initially preferred to fight the Persians and left for the east. He visited the front, but did not take any real action. He spent the winter of 360–361 in Antioch in Syria. There he faced the difficult decision whether to unleash a large-scale offensive on the Persians in the spring or turn his attention to the west, where Julian had begun to act like a real emperor and was readying himself to go to war with Constantius. Because the Persians retreated the choice was not a difficult one and, starting in the summer, Constantius focused all his energies on Julian.

The march westward was slow going. It was already November, not the ideal time to begin a major expedition, but no one dared to point that out to the emperor. They were barely underway when they came across the body of a man who had met a violent end. He lay on his right side and had no head. Because the body pointed towards the west, the emperor was gripped by fear. But instead of turning around, he pressed on at a greater speed. In Tarsus he came down with a fever. At first things did not look too bad, and he was able to resume his journey, until he came to Mopsucrenae, at the foot of the Taurus Mountains. The next day he wanted to continue on, but the high fever prevented that. In the days that followed, his condition worsened. According to Ammianus Marcellinus, who describes his death, this was because the high fever was drying out his veins. His body became so warm that no one could touch it. He glowed like an oven. There was no medical help. His breathing grew ever more faint, and he lamented his impending demise. He remained conscious till the very end. On his deathbed he named Julian as his successor. He had little choice. He had no children himself (after his death a daughter was born), and Julian was the only remaining member of the dynasty of Constantine.

His body was embalmed and placed in a coffin. Under the supervision of Jovian, head of the bodyguards, the emperor's remains were taken to Constantinople and interred at the Church of the

Holy Apostles. In the fourth and fifth centuries that spot would become the final resting place for many a Roman emperor.

Eutropius 10.15
Ammianus Marcellinus 21.15.1–4
Philostorgius 6.5
Zonaras 13.11

JULIAN
May/June 331–26/27 June 363
Emperor from February 360

With Julian, a man ascended the throne who had been marked by events in his early childhood. The memory of the liquidation of his relatives by the army in 337, which he and his brother Gallus had narrowly escaped, haunted him for the rest of his life. The fact that his Christian uncles Constantine, Constantius and Constans had allowed the murders to take place had a great influence on the formation of his ideas. He lost his Christian faith at a young age and fell under the spell of the Greek classics, although he did not declare his convictions at first. He immersed himself in ancient philosophy under the tutelage of Libanius, a leading orator and scholar, and other Greek professors. This only increased his distaste for Christianity. He considered the New Testament a literary work of little worth, which paled in comparison to the classics. His main interest was ancient paganism, into which he longed to breathe new life. Julian's religion was a mixture of philosophical tenets and old elements of the Roman state religion. He was a pantheist, who believed that the divine force was present throughout nature.

In 355 his studies were over and Julian stepped into the lime-light as sub-emperor, succeeding his murdered half-brother Gallus. He married Helena, the youngest sister of Constantius. His years in Gaul were very successful, and it was during that time that his imperial ambitions began to crystallise. We can only speculate what would have happened to Julian if Constantius had lived and an armed conflict would have had to determine who would ultimately be the lone ruler. Now with Constantius dead, the way was clear for him.

As emperor he could continue to shape his religious ideas and try to give them a political foundation. He did not reinstitute anti-Christian persecutions, though he did ban Christian teachers from instructing the young, confiscate churches and revoke priests' tax-exempt status. His break with the Christian policy of his predecessors earned him the nickname *Apostata* ('the Apostate') in the Christian world.

Julian did not have the time to make any lasting changes, as his reign was a short one, no longer than eighteen months. He was determined to push the Persians back over the Roman-drawn borders, and in 363 he marched on the city of Ctesiphon. He dismissed a peace offer from the Persians, and let himself be talked into undertaking a risky expedition, deep into the Persian Empire. The Persians employed guerrilla tactics, avoiding open confrontations. If only Julian had done the same. On the morning of what would be his last day, 26 or 27 June 363, he had been warned by Etruscan seers not to go into battle, as the falling star that he had seen the night before did not bode well for him. Though Julian was generally receptive to such warnings, he paid no heed to their words this time. At any rate, when he received word that his rear-guard was under attack he did not think for an instant about what the seers had advised him. At that moment he was riding at the head of his army, unarmed. In the excitement he had forgotten his armour, which his armour bearer had with him, and he rode towards the threatened rear-guard with his shield as his only protection. On the way there he heard that his left flank was being attacked by a mounted division, supported by elephants. He took immediate action and rode to the threatened flank. He managed to regroup his troops, and the Persians were forced to fall back.

Then he made a colossal mistake. Without any thought for his own safety, he called upon his soldiers to follow him and rode headlong into the multitude of fleeing Persians. His personal bodyguards, who had been separated from the emperor because of his quick actions, yelled for him to turn back, but he probably did not hear them. And then suddenly there was the spear, thrown by one of the enemy knights, that grazed his arm, pierced his side and lodged itself in his liver. Instinctively Julian tried to pull it out. In the process he cut the tendons of his fingers on the sharp barbs of the weapon and fell off his horse. The bodyguards who had rushed to his aid picked him up and brought him to the camp, where doctors tried to save his life. For a short time they seemed to be having some success. His pain diminished somewhat, and he took heart. He even asked for his weapons because he wanted to boost the soldiers' spirits with his presence. But there had been no real recovery and his strength rapidly declined. Weakened by loss of blood he could no longer sit up. The hope that he would pull through quickly vanished, particularly when he asked the name of the region in which he was now going to die and was given the answer: Phrygia. He had once heard that he would die in Phrygia, but he had always assumed the Phrygia in question was the one in Asia Minor.

His death was impressive, particularly in Ammianus Marcellinus' account, although we should be sceptical about the final speech the writer has the emperor make. With his grief-stricken friends and his most devoted officers assembled round his bed, Julian supposedly accounted for his actions, saying that he did not fear death and could bid farewell to life without fear. As those present wept, he said that it was beneath their dignity to mourn for an emperor who was favoured by heaven and the stars. He even wanted to engage the philosophers Maximus and Priscus, who were present, in a conversation about the divine nature of the soul, but his powers failed him. Blood flowed out of the wound in his lacerated side, and his swollen veins hindered his breathing. After drinking a glass of cold water he passed away peacefully, just thirty-two years old. The report from later Christian authors that he uttered the words, 'You have won, Galilean', should be relegated to the realm of fables.

The question of who killed Julian has often been asked, but no one has ever been able to come up with a satisfactory answer. The most obvious explanation is that the fatal spear was thrown by an unknown hand in the Persian lines. But it has also been suggested that a Christian soldier from the Roman ranks, disappointed by Julian's religious reforms, was the culprit.

Julian's remains were embalmed by the army and taken to Tarsus, where he was given a solemn burial. A century later Emperor Leo I decided that Julian deserved a final resting place alongside the other members of the dynasty of Constantine. In 457 he was interred in the Church of the Holy Apostles in Constantinople.

Ammianus Marcellinus 25.3
Libanius, *Orations* 18.274–275
Zosimus 3.29
Philostorgius 7.15
Zonaras 13.13

10

THE LATE
FOURTH CENTURY

JOVIAN
331–17 February 364
Emperor from 27 June 363

The morning after Julian's death, the highest-ranking generals met
to consider the question of who his successor should be. They looked
at various candidates, but differences in opinion between the generals from the west and those from the east made a quick decision
impossible. For a time it seemed as if Salutius, a political sym-
pathiser of Julian's, would be an acceptable candidate for everyone,
but he declined the offer owing to his age and poor health. While
discussions were still in progress, a number of soldiers in the camp
proclaimed Jovian emperor. For lack of a better alternative, the
army leadership made no protest.

Jovian, born in Moesia, was nothing like Julian; not in appearance, not in his military qualities and certainly not in the original-
ity of his ideas. He was a strong, somewhat heavy-set man with a
spotty education and a great appetite for food and drink. A devout
Christian, he had achieved few military successes of note. His
principal claim to fame was the fact he had been the one to bring
the remains of Emperor Constantius II to Constantinople.

The first thing Jovian did was make peace with the Persian king.
The conditions were not particularly favourable; the Empire had to
cede a number of provinces east of the Tigris. The summer heat, the
dust and the lack of water and provisions made the soldiers unwill-
ing and left him no other choice. The retreating army was split into
two. The larger of the two groups went to Tarsus, while the rest of
the army, including Jovian himself, went to Antioch. After a stay
of a few months he moved further west. In December he reached

Ankara. From there he wanted to continue on to Constantinople, but in Dadastana, on the border of Bithynia and Galatia, he was found dead in a house, with a red, swollen head. The cause of death is uncertain. Ammianus Marcellinus suggests various possibilities. He could have eaten too much – it is thought he might have consumed a large quantity of mushrooms – or perhaps he suffocated from inhaling smoke from a brazier, or maybe he was overcome by the fumes from a freshly painted wall in the bedroom. Because Ammianus Marcellinus' story compares Jovian's death to that of Scipio Aemilianus in the second century BC, the possibility of strangulation should not be ruled out.

Eutropius 10.18
Ammianus Marcellinus 25.10.11–13
Zosimus 3.35
Philostorgius 8.8

VALENTINIAN I
321–17 November 375
Emperor from 25 February 364

The new emperor was General Valentinian from Pannonia. At the insistence of the troops he appointed a co-emperor – not, as was expected, someone with a long record of service, but his own brother Valens. The agreement was that Valentinian would rule over Illyricum and the western provinces and Valens would be given control over the remaining Balkan provinces and the east. For a brief period in 365 it looked as if there might be a leadership crisis when both brothers fell ill, but they recovered and resumed their official duties. Valentinian resided in Milan from 366 onwards, and Valens returned to Constantinople.

Valentinian had to take immediate action against the Alamanni, who had invaded Gaul. On two separate occasions he crossed the Rhine and penetrated deep into enemy territory. He managed to contain them, though they came back a few more times, and it was not until 374 that a permanent peace could be brokered. The situation in Britain also demanded action. The Picts and the Scots were threatening the precarious peace. But Valentinian's general Theodosius, the father of the future emperor Theodosius I, defeated them and restored order. In 373–374 that same Theodosius was also successful in Mauretania, where the Moorish chief Firmus had rebelled and had been proclaimed emperor by the legions. He was no match for Theodosius' armies and eventually committed suicide.

Valentinian died a most unusual death. He was faced with incursions from the Quadi and Sarmatians, and in the summer of 375 he decided to organise a punitive expedition. After a few successful campaigns he made camp in Brigetio, one hundred kilometres west of Budapest. There he was visited by envoys from the Quadi, who had come to offer their surrender. But things turned out quite differently from how the emperor had expected. On the last night of his life he dreamed that he saw his wife with her hair down, dressed in mourning, getting ready to pay her final respects to him. Just before he was to receive the envoys, his horse reared up on its hind legs as he was about to mount it. The emperor was so angry that he ordered that the right hand of the stable boy who usually helped him on to his horse be cut off. The blameless youth did not survive.

His temper would ultimately prove to be his undoing. The Quadi were brought before him, and they begged forgiveness for their actions. They even offered recruits to solve the shortage of soldiers. But at a certain point Valentinian suddenly flew into a rage. Their remark that the construction of a fortified stronghold on their territory was excessive pushed the emperor over the edge. Ammianus Marcellinus tells us what happened next. He does not recount exactly what it was that Valentinian said to the Quadi, but the essence of his words was that they should be grateful to the Romans for being so obliging. After a while he calmed down and seemed to be more receptive to their arguments. But his inner rage had already done its destructive work. All of a sudden he looked as if he had been struck by lightning. His throat closed up; he lost the ability to speak and his face turned a fiery red. His pulse grew faint, his breathing became laboured and he broke out in a sweat. He had apparently suffered a stroke or a heart attack on the spot.

His servants led him away and put him to bed. He remained conscious and observed everyone who was present, fearful that a potential murderer would make use of the confusion to kill him. There was a frantic search for a doctor. It was some time before one could be found, because Valentinian had sent all the doctors out to attend to sick and wounded soldiers. The doctor tried to stimulate the emperor's circulation by bleeding him, but without success. No matter where he pricked his veins, he could not find a drop of blood. Valentinian tried to say something, but he had lost the ability to speak. His body convulsed; he hiccuped and hacked; he gnashed his teeth and his fists punched helplessly at the air. A short time later he expired.

The matter of succession seemed simple enough. His son Gratian, to whom he had already given the title Augustus in 367, was the obvious choice. Because Gratian was in Trier at the time and there was a fear that if the new ruler was away too long it might put the loyalty of the army to Valentinian's family under serious strain, another son, Valentinian, who was just four years old, was named emperor as well.

Ammianus Marcellinus 30.6

Zosimus 4.17

Socrates Scholasticus, *Ecclesiastical Histories* 4.31

VALENS
c. 328–9 August 378
Emperor from 28 March 364

Co-emperor Valens was not having such an easy time of it either. Procopius, a general, had had himself proclaimed emperor in September 365 in Constantinople and had acquired support for his bid for power from a number of Gothic tribes. Valens was on the point of resuming hostilities with the Persians, who were showing little regard for the agreements they had made with Jovian, and he immediately left Antioch for Constantinople. Procopius was soon defeated in May 366 and realised that he would no longer be able to play any significant role. His troops realised that as well. They took him prisoner and turned him over to Valens, who promptly had him beheaded.

Valens was unable to keep the Persians permanently in check. Negotiations were fruitless, and in 376, when he was readying himself for a major expedition against them, he received news that the Visigoths had risen up against him. A few years before, he had given them permission to settle in the Empire, in Thrace, considering that the Roman legions were too weak to put the Goths out of action for good and that allowing them into the army would mean a welcome reinforcement. Things did not go as Valens had expected, however. The Visigoths had not been sufficiently integrated into the various subdivisions of the army in time, and local officials exploited them in a scandalous fashion. Riots broke out, and the Ostrogoths profited from this state of affairs by also invading the Empire. Valens deemed military action advisable.

On 9 August 378 the decisive battle took place, at Adrianopolis. Valens had not listened to his advisers, who recommended waiting for reinforcements from Gratian. Under a blazing sun and amid clouds of dust the Romans advanced on the enemy camp. At two o'clock they were able to make out the carts that the Goths had positioned in a circle around the camp. The Roman army approached, in battle array. The Goths were initially frightened by the clatter of arms and the fact that the support they had been promised had not arrived. Negotiations between Valens and the Goth leader Fritigern broke down. For the Roman soldiers the heat became unbearable when the Goths started lighting fires and the wind blew the warm smoke in their direction. Valens saw that the situation was becoming unstable and decided to accept the Goths' demand that he turn over a few prominent persons to them as hostages and thus prevent an armed conflict. But the tension was too much for a number of archers, who fired their arrows at the enemy. In no time both armies were locked in a life and death struggle. For a while it looked as if the left flank of the Roman army would be able to force its way into the enemy camp, but because support from the cavalry failed to arrive, the assault lost momentum. They got separated from the rest of the army and had no chance against the hordes that descended upon them.

It soon became clear that the Romans were losing on all fronts. They were trapped between Gothic cavalry, who had ridden around the Roman ranks, and the advancing foot soldiers. They put up a valiant defence and killed a large number of enemy soldiers, but defeat was inevitable. Their lines were broken up and enemy archers aimed their deadly arrows at the Romans as they fled in panic. Thousands – the exact number is unknown – lost their lives on the battlefield. Less than a third of the army managed to escape.

Valens was one of those who got away, making his way over masses of corpses to an army unit that had managed to hold out. But when assistance from auxiliary troops that Valens had been keeping in reserve failed to materialise, everyone took to his heels, pursued by the Goths. The roads they used to make their escape were strewn with dead soldiers and horses. In the early morning Valens perished in the midst of the common soldiers, mortally wounded by an arrow. At least, this is the official version, but anyone who could have witnessed it would have died as well. Another story in circulation has the wounded Valens being carried off the battlefield by his bodyguards and brought to a fortified estate. While he was being treated there the house was surrounded by the enemy, who were unaware the emperor was inside. They first tried to break open the doors, which were locked and barred, but they abandoned this idea when they were met by a hail of arrows from inside the house. They gathered straw and branches, bundled them together, lit the bundles and threw the burning torches at the house. The emperor reportedly died in the flames. The source of the story is one of his bodyguards, who jumped out of a window and managed to escape.

Ammianus Marcellinus 31.13
Zosimus 4.24
Jordanes 26.138
Socrates Scholasticus, *Ecclesiastical Histories* 4.38
Zonaras 13.16

GRATIAN
18 April 359–25 August 383
Emperor from 24 August 367

Gratian was now the only true Roman emperor; Valentinian II was still much too young to handle the responsibilities of government. But Gratian realised that he was not able to rule the Empire on his own. The combined threats of the Goths, the Alamanni and the Franks would give pretenders to the throne the chance to seize power. Therefore he appointed a general, Theodosius, co-emperor. This took some persuading, as Theodosius had decided some years before to retire to the seclusion of his estate in Spain, after his father, the successful general Theodosius, had been indicted and executed. On 19 January 379 he was crowned co-emperor in Sirmium by Gratian.

Theodosius avoided further battles with the Goths, eventually making peace with them in 382. The terms of the peace stipulated that the Visigoths would get land in the Balkans and could live there as a nation under their own rulers and laws. Under a treaty they were bound (*foederati*) to the Roman Empire. Rome had to pay their wages and provide for their upkeep, while the Visigoths in turn were required to serve in the Roman army. For a time this was a felicitous solution, but in the long term it would lead to a weakening of the army and to social turmoil.

From 381 onwards Gratian's primary residence was Milan, where he often associated with Christian intellectuals, among them Bishop Ambrose, the renowned church father. In June 383, however, he was forced to take military action against the Alamanni, who had invaded Gaul. He crossed the Brenner Pass and entered Gaul, but the expedition ended in disaster. It was not the Alamanni who were to blame, but the seasoned soldiers of the legions in Britain. For some time they had been annoyed that Gratian did not value their accomplishments and showed a greater appreciation for the archers of the auxiliary troops. In the spring of 383 they proclaimed their commander Maximus emperor. Shortly thereafter they crossed into Gaul. The Rhine legions immediately joined up with the rebels, while the Gallic troops initially remained loyal to Gratian. But his almost anti-militaristic conduct made them change their tune. When, during the first skirmishes in the vicinity of Paris, he showed no real interest in military strategy, they defected, along with their general Merobaudes. Gratian had no choice but to sound the retreat. Together with a small company of cavalrymen he tried to make it to the Alps. To his disappointment the cities of Gaul refused to open their gates to him. After crossing the Rhône he was at his wits' end. He saw no other possibility but to give himself up to Andragathius, the commander of the army unit that was hot on his trail. He hoped that his life would be spared, but he was killed almost immediately at the house where Andragathius was staying, on 25 August 383. His body was brought to Maximus, who kept it as a trophy. It is unknown how long it remained there. Bishop Ambrose hints in one of his letters that he went to Trier in 386 to negotiate the release of Gratian's remains with Maximus, and with success, he claims. Gratian reportedly found his final resting place in Milan.

Rufinus 11.14
Jerome, *Epistulae* 60.15
Zosimus 4.34–35
Ambrose, *Epistulae* 24

MAXIMUS
?–28 August 388
Emperor from the spring of 383

Maximus resided in Trier, but there was still Valentinian II in the west as well. To be sure, he was just twelve years old, but he enjoyed the protection of Theodosius in the east. Maximus was well aware of this, and he therefore tried to win the boy emperor over to his side. He invited him to come to Trier and live with him 'as father and son'. Bishop Ambrose managed to stop Valentinian from accepting the invitation. Theodosius realised that a war against Maximus and his well-trained troops would be a risky undertaking and accepted Maximus as co-emperor in 384, albeit with great reluctance. The agreement was that Valentinian II would keep his own sphere of influence in Italy, Africa and Illyricum while Maximus would reign over Gaul, Spain and Britain.

In the summer of 387 Maximus felt that the time had come to put an end to Valentinian's reign, and he invaded Italy. Together with his mother and a large number of courtiers Valentinian fled to Thessaloniki, which was situated in the part of the Empire controlled by Theodosius. The latter promptly demanded that Valentinian be restored to the throne, but Maximus ignored the request. After consulting the Senate in Constantinople, Theodosius organised a great expedition 'for the liberation of the west'. Maximus was attacked by land and by sea. He managed to avoid a naval confrontation, but he was completely surprised by Theodosius' swift overland advance. He retreated to Aquileia, but quickly realised that his remaining men would not be able to defend the city against Theodosius' superior numbers. Perhaps he attempted a sortie, but that must have failed, since in August 388 he surrendered to the advance guard of Theodosius' army, which had by then entered the city. He was stripped of his imperial medals and led away to Theodosius' camp in shackles. For a time it seemed as if the latter would grant him clemency and spare his life, but when the soldiers insisted on killing Maximus, he consented. They dragged Maximus away and handed him over to his executioners. On 28 August 388 Maximus was beheaded after being subjected to horrendous torture. His head was put on display in the camp as a deterrent to other pretenders to the throne.

Chronica Minora I, pp. 245, 388
Zosimus 4, 46

VALENTINIAN II
371–15 May 392
Emperor from 22 November 375

Valentinian was restored to the rank of emperor that same year, 388. But he was no match for the machinations of two Frankish advisers, Bauto and Arbogast, particularly the latter, who, as *magister militum* ('supreme general'), did as he pleased. In the spring of 392 the emperor gave him his notice, but Arbogast coolly replied that he had not been appointed by him and therefore could not be dismissed by him.

On 15 May the emperor was found dead in Vienne in Gaul. According to Zosimus, Arbogast killed him with his own hands. This allegedly happened when Valentinian was out playing with friends near the city walls, completely unaware that danger was just around the corner. Arbogast purportedly leapt upon him and struck him dead, killing the emperor almost instantly. According to other sources he was murdered by eunuchs, working on orders from Arbogast. There are also stories that Arbogast disposed of him by means of a ruse. To eliminate the traces of his crime he strung him up on a length of rope so that his death would look like a suicide.

Zosimus 4.54
Orosius 7.35
Philostorgius 11.1
John of Antioch, Fragment 187
Socrates Scholasticus, *Ecclesiastical Histories* 5.25

EUGENIUS
?–6 September 394
Emperor from 22 August 392

Because Arbogast knew he had no chance at the throne, he arranged for Eugenius, a professor of rhetoric, to become the new emperor. Although the latter did not have a military background, he achieved impressive results in the wars against the Alamanni and the Franks. But Theodosius would not hear of sharing the emperorship with Eugenius, and on 23 January 393 he appointed his eight-year-old son Honorius co-emperor. A year later he left Constantinople with a large army and set off for the west, determined to deal with Eugenius once and for all. The decisive confrontation took place on 5 September 394, on the banks of the river Frigidus (Wippach), on the border between Italy and Slovenia. According to the sources the battle raged for two days, with enormous losses on both sides. The Christian authors speak of a fight between the forces of light (the Christian Theodosius) and of darkness (the pagans Eugenius and

Arbogast). The banners with the likeness of Hercules and the images of the lightning-slinging Jupiter in Eugenius' army were no match for a solar eclipse and a sudden storm, which apparently worked to Theodosius' advantage and helped him to victory. Eugenius was arrested a day after the battle after attempting to flee and brought to Theodosius in shackles. He threw himself at his feet and begged for mercy, but the soldiers chopped his head off before Theodosius was able to make a decision. The head was stuck on a long pole and carried around the camp in triumph.

Arbogast fled into the mountains and committed suicide when he realised that he had no reason to expect clemency from Theodosius.

Zosimus 4.58
Socrates Scholasticus, *Ecclesiastical Histories* 5.25
Philostorgius 11.2
John of Antioch, Fragment 187

THEODOSIUS I
11 January 347–17 January 395
Emperor from 19 January 379

Theodosius was now the sole sovereign. Although he had shown himself in the west a few times to wage wars against border nations and to dispatch pretenders to the throne, he spent the majority of his reign in the east, mainly in Constantinople, where he occupied much of his time with religious matters. Two years before his final confrontation with Eugenius, he had proclaimed Christianity the state religion. He banned all pagan rituals, an act which Christians equated with a legitimisation of hard action against the pagans. The situation would often get out of hand, when throngs of Christians took to the streets and pulled down pagan statues, as happened in Alexandria, where a local bishop organised the siege and eventual destruction of a shrine to the Egyptian god Serapis. The pagans were placed in the same position as the Christians had been during the

143

persecutions of the third century. They were forced to convert to Christianity on the threat of violence. A small number of pagans stood firm, but high-ranking Romans increasingly converted, less out of religious conviction than for the sake of their careers.

The removal of Eugenius was Theodosius' last accomplishment. He died four months later, on 17 January 395, probably in Milan. A few weeks earlier he had become seriously ill. During the games that were held to add lustre to his presence in the city he became unwell and had to leave the stadium. He died not long afterwards. It is also possible that he died on the trip back to Constantinople. Dropsy has been suggested as a possible cause of death. His body was taken to Constantinople, where it was solemnly interred on 8 November in the imperial vault in the Church of the Holy Apostles.

Ambrose, *The Death of Theodosius* 18
Socrates Scholasticus, *Ecclesiastical Histories* 5.26
Philostorgius 11.2

11

THE DIVIDED EMPIRE

Theodosius left the Empire to his two sons. Arcadius, almost eighteen years old, became the ruler of the eastern part, while the ten-year-old Honorius reigned in the west. In actuality the division was along linguistic lines, separating the Latin west from the Greek-Hellenistic east. From the outset it was clear that Arcadius had got the better end of the deal. In the conflicts with the Goths the emperors of the east hardly had to give up any territory, and there had been no major organisational changes in that part of the Empire either. The central government, the provincial and local authorities, commercial life and the economy were not significantly affected. The west, which had never reached the high level of development enjoyed by the east, lacked the urban network that made effective government possible. The crisis of the third century had left deep scars, and the tightly regimented society of the fourth century had clearly exposed the contrasts between the rich senatorial elite and the rest of the population. There were also differences in the military. The west was dependent on Germans from outside the Empire for new troops, while in the east the strength of the army could be maintained by drafting men from the Balkans, Asia Minor and Armenia.

ARCADIUS
377/378–1 May 408
Emperor of the Eastern Roman Empire from 17 January 395

Arcadius was served by a number of advisers who were much more intelligent than he, but also much more cunning. The prefect of the imperial guard, Rufinus, and an older eunuch, Eutropius, had the emperor in their power for some time. In addition he also fell victim to the intrigues of his wife Eudoxia, who was his superior in every way. It was thanks to the new commander of the imperial guard, Anthemius, that the Eastern Roman Empire remained organisationally intact and was spared any invasions from enemies outside its borders. On 1 May 408 the emperor suddenly died, just thirty-one years old. The cause of death is unknown, but it is generally assumed that he died of natural causes. He has gone down in history as an ineffectual, colourless figure, a short and skinny man unknown to the ordinary residents of Constantinople. No protests were heard when his son Theodosius II, who was just seven years old, succeeded him.

Zosimus 5.34
Socrates Scholasticus, *Ecclesiastical Histories* 6.23

HONORIUS
9 September 384–27 August 423
Emperor of the Western Roman Empire from 23 January 395

Honorius was just like his brother, weak and timid and dependent on advisers who set his policies. In his case these advisers were German generals, the most influential of whom was Stilicho, who was married to one of Theodosius' nieces and had been supreme commander of the army during the last years of his reign. In actuality it was Stilicho who made policy and wielded power. However, his attempts to seize power in the east ended in failure. A dispute arose between the west and the east over the territory of Illyria. Stilicho felt the entire territory should belong to the west, although Theodosius, in dividing the Empire, had split it into two. Alaric, the king of the Visigoths, who were living in Thrace as *foederati*, believed he could profit from this disagreement and occupied Moesia, north of Illyria. Visigoth raids caused considerable damage in the Balkans, but they could not take the fortified cities. The Romans under Stilicho won small victories over the Visigoths on two occasions, though they were unable to finish them off completely.

After 405 the situation in the west deteriorated rapidly. In December 406 the German Vandals and the Suebi, who were being pushed westward under pressure from the Huns, broke through the Rhine line. They were followed not long afterwards by the Burgundians. Alaric's decision to go to Italy with his Visigoths in 408 forced Honorius to face the full brunt of the German problem. The Visigoths plundered their way through Greece and after crossing through Illyria they headed north, in the direction of Italy. The first city they captured was Aquileia, on the northern coast of the Adriatic Sea. After that they threatened Milan, the seat of Honorius' government, forcing the emperor to flee to Ravenna, which could be defended more easily. His attempts to mount a punitive expedition against them came to nothing, but he refused their request for fertile land in central Europe. At that point the Visigoths headed for Rome. Perhaps they could have been persuaded to change their plans, but on 23 August 408 the execution of the Roman general Stilicho, who had since fallen from grace but whom the Visigoths respected, prevented that. They entered Rome on two separate occasions. When the Senate refused to pay for their withdrawal they invaded Rome once again, on 24 August 410, wreaking havoc there for three days before continuing on into Italy.

The conquest of Rome must have come as an enormous shock. It may well have been the most shocking event of the fifth century. For the inhabitants of Rome the invasion of the Visigoths was a new low in the history of their city, even though the occupation had only lasted three days. Intellectuals saw the taking of the city as a symbol of decline and decay. The mighty capital of the Roman Empire, which had been unthreatened for eight centuries – the only time Rome had ever been captured was in 389 BC, by the Gauls, and the Carthaginian Hannibal and his forces had stood at the city gates in 218 BC – had fallen prey to barbarian troops. The myth of the eternal city had been shattered. For centuries the appellation *Roma aeterna* had been symbolic of the political and cultural significance of the Roman Empire. Even during the troubled times of the third and fourth centuries, people continued to believe in that myth. For this reason the occupation of Rome was particularly hard to take.

The fall of Rome did not have any short-term repercussions. The death of King Alaric and the desire of most Visigoths for good farmland spared Rome a prolonged occupation. The Visigoths left Italy and went to Gaul, only to leave again almost immediately for the territory to the north and south of the Pyrenees, where they founded their own state, with Toulouse as its capital. The capture of Rome did, however, usher in a number of developments that would, over the long term, lead to catastrophic upheaval within the Roman Empire.

In addition to the Germans, Honorius also had his hands full dealing with several pretenders, who thought they could make use of the German invasions to seize power. In the spring of 407 the legions in Britain proclaimed their general Constantine emperor. He crossed the Channel and managed to extend his authority to Gaul and Spain. Two years later the senator Priscus Attalus also had himself proclaimed emperor in Rome, but Alaric's capture of the city put an end to his aspirations. That same year Maximus was presented with the purple vestments in Spain. Honorius' general Constantius ended the ambitions of the pretender in Britain as well as the one in Spain. In 413 he put down a second rebellion in Gaul, under the leadership of Jovinus. General Constantius evidently made such a good impression on Honorius that the latter offered him his sister Galla Placidia in marriage in 417. In 421 he even appointed him co-emperor. Constantius did not have long to enjoy his newly acquired rank, as he died just seven months later. He had one son, Valentinian III, who would later become emperor.

In August 423 Honorius died, probably from dropsy or lung oedema. There is little positive that can be said about his reign. He came to the throne as a child and always remained a child, forever dependent on the advice of others. He was a weak personality, who was dominated by fear and ducked out of difficult tasks. He had to look on as Rome was sacked and territories were lost, and he was threatened by numerous pretenders to the throne. Even so, he managed to stay in power for nearly thirty years. There were better emperors who had done a lot worse.

Philostorgius 12.13
Socrates Scholasticus, Ecclesiastical Histories 7.22
Chronica Minora I, pp. 470, 658

THEODOSIUS II
10 April 401–28 July 450
Emperor of the Eastern Roman Empire from 10 January 408

In Constantinople power passed from the weakling Arcadius to the child Theodosius II in 408. Initially he was under the thumb of Anthemius, the commander of the imperial guard, but after his death in 414, when the emperor was just thirteen, Theodosius II began to go his own way, although it cannot be denied that his sister Pulcheria tried her best to impose her views on the emperor and was sometimes quite successful at it. She fought bitterly with Eudocia, Theodosius' beautiful and highly educated wife, for the political favour of the emperor. Pulcheria ultimately won out, and Eudocia was forced to retire from public life.

Theodosius may not have been a strong personality, but he was an intelligent and artistic man, who surrounded himself with outstanding advisers and capable generals. In addition to that he had the good fortune that the political situation remained manageable, despite repeated incursions by the Huns in the Balkan provinces. They could only be bought off with huge sums of money. In 447 the Roman army suffered a major defeat at the hands of the Huns under Attila. The result was that large annual tributes had to be paid to keep their aggression in check.

Theodosius is most associated with the publication of the *Codex Theodosianus*, a digest of laws from the third century onward. The codex, which was published in 438, was greeted with enthusiasm in the Senates of Rome and Constantinople. He intended for the codex to be enlarged with new legislation in the future. To underscore this aim he added some laws himself.

The last years of his reign must have brought Theodosius little joy. The real power in the palace was in the hands of a eunuch, Chrysaphius. The emperor signed important documents without reading them. With the help of Pulcheria, Chrysaphius was removed from the scene, but the emperor was not given the time to re-establish his authority. On 26 July 450, three months after the eunuch was deposed, the emperor went out horseback riding. Near the river Lycus, not far from the city, he fell. It is likely he broke his back or neck in the fall, leaving him paralysed; he died two days later. On his deathbed the childless Theodosius named Marcian, a high-ranking officer who had earned his spurs in various military expeditions, as his successor with the words, 'It has been revealed to me that you shall rule after me.' It was probably Pulcheria who had arranged the succession, in the expectation that Marcian would take her as his wife and she would be able to maintain her position of power.

John Malalas 14
Chronicon Paschale, Anno 450
Zonaras 13.24

VALENTINIAN III
419–16 March 455
Emperor of the Western Roman Empire from 23 October 425

In the west a complex situation had arisen following the death of Honorius. His sister Galla Placidia, who was married to Constantius, wanted her son Valentinian III to succeed Honorius. Because Honorius had not made any arrangements prior to his death, Theodosius in Constantinople considered himself to be the only legitimate Roman emperor. He only changed his opinion and bet on Valentinian when a high-ranking civil servant, Johannes, was proclaimed emperor in Rome, a move that was supported by a number of prominent individuals, including General Aetius, a Roman from Moesia. The troops invaded Ravenna, where Johannes had taken cover. He was captured, ridiculed and gruesomely mutilated. Afterwards he was placed on a donkey and led through the theatre of Aquileia, where he was eventually beheaded. The road was now open for Valentinian III. To affirm the ties to his family, Theodosius II betrothed his daughter Eudoxia to the six-year-old Valentinian III.

If Honorius himself was not a forceful figure, his nephew was a spoiled libertine. According to the sources he let himself be guided by magicians and soothsayers. He left political affairs to others. When he reached the age of discretion, the only thing for which he showed a more than normal interest was religion. During his reign the power and the authority of Pope Leo I, the bishop of Rome, grew, as did the political influence of Aetius, the latter to the great annoyance of Galla Placidia, who had not forgotten that Aetius had supported Johannes' *coup d'état*.

Valentinian and Aetius could only look on as the Empire continued to crumble. North Africa was lost to the Vandals; the Suebi controlled the north-west of Spain, and in Gaul the Visigoths, Burgundians and Franks were in power. The only success Rome had was against the Huns under Attila. In a great battle on the Catalaunian Fields (in the vicinity of Châlons-sur-Marne) the Huns were defeated. They retreated but returned a year later and invaded northern Italy. There a meeting took place between Attila and Pope Leo. There is no record of what was said there, but the result of their conversation was a Hun withdrawal. A year later Attila died and the Hun Empire disintegrated.

The successes against the Huns bolstered Aetius' position. A few of his opponents were envious of his success and urged the emperor to get rid of his adviser. Valentinian listened to them and condemned his general to death. The way in which the sentence was carried out says a great deal about Valentinian's base nature. On 21 September 454 Aetius came to the palace to place a piece of legislation before the emperor. Suddenly the latter sprang from his throne and accused Aetius of treason. Before he could utter a word in his own defence, the emperor rushed at him with his sword drawn. Together with his chamberlain, the eunuch Heraclius, he slew the defenceless Aetius.

Vengeance came swiftly. Heraclius managed to convince the emperor that it was not in his interest to appoint someone to replace Aetius. This was not to the liking of Maximus, a high-ranking Roman and one of the instigators of Aetius' murder. He also had personal reasons for his actions: Maximus was angry at Valentinian for allegedly seducing his wife. Maximus now planned another assassination, and this time the emperor was the target. He chose two former servants of Aetius, the Scythians Optila and Thraustila, whom he knew were still incensed over the unjust fate of their master. The emperor, however, was unaware of this. On 16 March 455 he rode out to the Field of Mars with a small group of bodyguards, including Optila and Thraustila. When he dismounted and picked up his bow to take part in a shooting competition, the two men attacked him. Optila struck him on the temple with his sword. The emperor turned around to see what miscreant had done such a thing. Optila struck again, this time hitting the emperor full in the face. He died on the spot. Thraustila beat Heraclius to death. Afterwards they grabbed the imperial diadem and Valentinian's horse and hurried to Maximus, who rewarded them with a military promotion.

John of Antioch, Fragment 201
Gregory of Tours, *Histories* 2.8

MAXIMUS
c. 395–2 June 455
Emperor of the Western Roman Empire from 17 March 455

Rome waited in anxious anticipation to see who would be Valentinian's successor. There were various candidates, but none of them really stood out. First of all there was Maximus, then there was Maximian, the son of a wealthy merchant from Egypt, and finally Majorian, an army commander with a good reputation.

Maximus came out on top. On 17 March, one day after the murder of Valentinian, he became the new emperor. The fact that he had few scruples in his pursuit of power was reconfirmed when he forced Eudoxia, Valentinian's widow, to marry him immediately, an act that should be seen as an attempt to ally himself with the imperial family.

But things did not work out quite as he had hoped. According to the Byzantine chronicler Malchus, Eudoxia called upon the king of the Vandals, Gaiseric, to take revenge, a detail that is not mentioned by other writers. In any case, at the end of May Gaiseric appeared at the mouth of the Tiber with a huge fleet and made camp ten kilometres outside the city. Maximus was in no position to lead the resistance to Gaiseric and tried to flee before the Vandals entered the city. He leapt on to a horse and rode to one of the city gates. But his flight did not go unnoticed. He was showered with abuse and pelted with stones. Just before he reached the gate he was hit square on his temple by a stone. He fell off his horse and was lynched by the disenchanted populace and the embittered soldiers. His body was torn to pieces and thrown into the Tiber. He had been emperor for just seventy days. Two days after his death the Vandals entered Rome and ravaged the city. They took everything in the palace they could get their hands on; even statues did not escape their rapacity. After fourteen days Gaiseric left again, with a great deal of plunder and a number of senators as prisoners. Eudoxia and her daughter of the same name were taken along to north Africa as well. He treated the mother with great respect and gave the daughter to his son Huneric in marriage.

Chronica Minora I, p. 663
Jordanes, *Historia Romana* 334
John of Antioch, Fragment 201

AVITUS
c. 395–17/18 October 456 or later
Emperor of the Western Roman Empire from
10 July 455 to 17/18 October 456

Once again Rome was left behind in confusion. Avitus, a descendent of a Roman senatorial family from Auvergne in Gaul, took full advantage of that. He had held a number of senior military posts and was known to be reliable and trustworthy. It is hard to say what made him decide to make a bid for the emperorship. Perhaps he got carried away by listening to the king of the Visigoths, Theoderic. Avitus was at that moment in Gaul. In Arles he was proclaimed emperor on 10 July 455 in the presence of Theoderic and his Visigoths. Three months later he was still in Gaul, probably to assure himself of sufficient support. After arriving in Italy he tried to make direct contact with the emperor in the east, Marcian, and to reach some sort of agreement with Majorian and Ricimer, the generals of the Roman armies in Italy. The emperor did not respond, and the latter two refused to co-operate and openly rebelled. Helped by the food shortage in Rome, which Avitus could do nothing about, they forced the emperor, who was unpopular with both the Senate and the people, to leave the city in January 456.

It is unclear what happened to Avitus after that. According to John of Antioch, Majorian and Ricimer attacked the fugitive emperor. He saw no way out but to take refuge in a church, give up his crown and wait and see what his enemies intended to do with him. But they wanted to get rid of him for good. They left only after learning that Avitus had died of hunger and thirst or at the hands of assassins they had sent to strangle him. Other writers have questioned this version. They tell of a military encounter taking place on 17 or 18 October 456 between Avitus' men and Ricimer's troops. The latter won and slaughtered Avitus' supporters. The life of the emperor was spared, however, and he was ordained bishop of Piacenza by Bishop Eusebius of Milan. But even here he was not safe from Majorian and the Senate. He fled to Clermont in Gaul, where he hoped to be safe, but he died *en route* in Brioude. He was buried in the Church of St Julian. The exact date of his death is unknown, but it was some time between the end of 456 and the middle of 457.

John of Antioch, Fragment 202
Gregory of Tours, *Histories* 2.11
Jordanes, *Getica* 45.240
Chronica Minora I, p. 304

MARCIAN
c. 392–27 January 457
Emperor of the Eastern Roman Empire from 25 August 450

In Constantinople Marcian became emperor of the east one month after the death of Theodosius II. The only thing we know about his background is that he came from Thrace or Illyria and had made a name for himself in the army. Later stories describe his being taken prisoner by the Vandals around the year 430. King Gaiseric was supposedly so impressed by him that he predicted he would one day become emperor.

Upon taking office he broke with the policy of his predecessor and cut off all payments to the Huns. They were too weak to object. Because Marcian no longer had to wage any costly wars on the eastern border, the financial position of the state greatly improved, with the result that wealth taxes, which were levied mainly on rich senators, could be abolished, a move that boosted Marcian's popularity. Like his predecessor he had an interest in religion. He played an active role in mediating between orthodox believers and dissenters in questions of faith. He acquired his greatest renown with the Council of Chalcedon, which he organised in 451. At the council heretical movements were condemned and orthodoxy was declared the only true faith.

After a reign that was generally considered a blessing for the Eastern Roman Empire, Marcian died, at the age of sixty-five. He had been having problems with his feet for some time, possibly the result of gangrene. In early January the condition worsened. His feet began to mortify and he could barely walk. But Marcian fulfilled the tasks of government and discharged his representative duties as if nothing were the matter. On the evening of 26 January 457 he insisted on participating in a procession to commemorate the victims of an earthquake in Constantinople ten years before. The route that the procession would cover was long, approximately twelve kilometres. Marcian did not flinch, and in accordance with custom he distributed gifts to spectators along the way. But he suddenly became unwell; he lost consciousness and was taken to the palace. He died there the next day. He was buried in the Church of the Holy Apostles, next to Pulcheria, whom he had married a short time after ascending the throne and who had died four years before.

Theodorus Lector, *Ecclesiastical History* 1.7
Chronica Minora I, p. 305; II, pp. 30, 87

MAJORIAN
c. 420–2/7 August 461
Emperor of the Western Roman Empire from 457

Almost simultaneously a power vacuum had opened up in both the west and the east. In the east, Leo I, a fifty-six-year-old Thracian from Dacia, was appointed emperor quite soon after the death of Marcian; in the west it took several months before a successor could be found. Initially it was mainly Ricimer, a barbarian with Suebi and Visigoth blood in his veins, who profited from the absence of a legitimate emperor. In the months leading up to Majorian's appointment he was the one calling the shots, and even after Majorian's accession he remained in power as a sort of 'co-regent'.

The exact date of Majorian's appointment is not known. It must have taken place some time between 18 February and 27 December 457. Once in power, Marjorian did everything to distinguish himself and show that he was not just Ricimer's puppet. At first his authority extended only as far as the Italian frontier, but he later succeeded in restoring Roman authority to parts of Gaul and Spain.

The preparations for an expedition against the Vandals in north Africa ushered in his downfall. In 460 he wanted to make the crossing from Spain with a fleet of three hundred ships, but near Carthagena his ships were raided by the Vandals and a portion of his fleet was destroyed or sunk. Majorian sounded the retreat and wanted to return to Italy. He stayed in Arles for a while, dissolved his army and, accompanied by only a few bodyguards, left for Rome. He never arrived, however. Ricimer, who had helped him put an end to the reign of Avitus five years before, had acquired new favourites in his absence. There was no place in his future plans for Majorian, who had followed his own counsel while in Gaul and Spain. Ricimer turned out with a military force and arrested Majorian in the vicinity of Tortona in Liguria. The most probable date is 2 August 461. What followed was the total humiliation of the emperor. His imperial garments and diadem were taken from him, he was beaten, kicked and tortured and finally, a few days later, beheaded by the river Ira. Ricimer put out the story that Majorian had died of dysentery. He was the last Western Roman emperor whose authority extended beyond the Italian border.

John of Antioch, Fragment 203
Jordanes, *Getica* 45.236
Procopius, *The Vandal War* 1.7
Chronica Minora I, p. 305

LIBIUS SEVERUS
?–after 25 September 465
Emperor of the Western Roman Empire from 19 November 461

It would be another three months before there was a new emperor. The choice eventually fell to Libius Severus, a Lucanian who was officially appointed by the Senate in Ravenna through Ricimer's intercession. Because Emperor Leo in Constantinople refused to recognise him, he reigned as a puppet of Ricimer, who was the real power behind the throne. Because his authority was far from undisputed, he had to defend his position from rivals almost continuously. The most important of these was Aegidius in Gaul. He managed to hold out for three years, but he was killed in 465.

However, Severus did not survive him by long. He died following a reign of nearly four years, some time in the fall of 465. There is some disagreement in the sources as to the circumstances of his death. It is possible that Ricimer, who had experience in eliminating emperors he himself had helped into the throne, was involved in his death in some way because Libius Severus had begun to show too much independence of judgement. According to this version he supposedly poisoned the emperor in his palace. But it is equally possible that Severus died of natural causes. Also we should not rule out the possibility that Emperor Leo, who wanted better relations with the west and therefore wanted Severus out of the way, had had a hand in his death.

Chronica Minora I, p. 305
Sidonius Apollinaris, *Carmina* 2.317–318

ANTHEMIUS
c. 420–11 July 472
Emperor of the Western Roman Empire from 12 April 467

Rome entered another emperorless period. This did not bother Ricimer, because it meant that he was once again in charge. But in the end he had to consent to the appointment of a new candidate by Leo in Constantinople: Anthemius, born in Constantinople and named after his maternal grandfather, who had played such a prominent role at the imperial court of Arcadius and Theodosius II from 405 to 411. On 12 April 467 he made his entrance into Rome at the head of a great army and was solemnly proclaimed emperor. Anthemius had no easy task ahead of him. With the exception of Italy, the west was dominated by barbarian nations, who were showing less and less respect for Rome. The great question upon his accession was how he, a Greek, would be able to get along with Ricimer. Initially things seemed to go well, and Anthemius even gave Ricimer his daughter Alypia in marriage. But Anthemius had his own generals and advisers and did not plan on blindly following the dictates of the 'kingmaker'. And, what is more, he enjoyed the support of Emperor Leo.

After failed expeditions against the Vandals in north Africa and the Visigoths in Gaul, which resulted in the loss of even more territory, Anthemius lost the support of Ricimer. Father-in-law and son-in-law found themselves in direct opposition to each other. At first it was a war of words. Anthemius called Ricimer a barbarian and Ricimer in turn called the emperor a 'Greekling' and a 'Galatian'. But the situation soon turned violent. Early in 473 Ricimer left Rome for Milan, where he made preparations for a war against Anthemius. And once again he had his own candidate for the emperorship, this time Olybrius. Ricimer set off for Rome, lay siege to the city and blocked all supply routes. Anthemius managed to withstand the siege for a few months in the hope of reinforcements. When they failed to arrive, he was forced to fight. He lost, on 11 July 472, and this defeat sealed his fate. He himself knew that all too well, for Ricimer was not a man of mercy. His troops surrendered. He fled to the church of the martyr Chrysostomus (now the Church of Santa Maria in Trastevere) and mixed in with the beggars. But he was discovered in spite of his disguise. Gundobad, Ricimer's nephew, found him there and killed him. A tragic end for an emperor who had begun his reign with the best of intentions but was unable to cope with internal and external problems.

John Antioch, Fragment 209
Chronica Minora I, pp. 306, 746

OLYBRIUS
?–22 October/2 November 472
Emperor of the Western Roman Empire from April/May 472

Olybrius, scion of an old senatorial family, would be Ricimer's last emperor. He was a well-known figure in Rome, thanks to his marriage to Placidia, daughter of Emperor Valentinian III. After Rome had been taken by the Vandals she and her mother had been brought to north Africa; they were later released. His candidacy was also backed by Gaiseric, the king of the Vandals, and this was the very reason Leo wanted him out of the picture. He hatched a truly treacherous plan. He sent Olybrius to Rome, ostensibly to reconcile Ricimer and Anthemius, in reality to have Olybrius eliminated. He sent a letter to Anthemius requesting him to kill Olybrius immediately upon his arrival. However, the letter was intercepted and fell into the hands of Ricimer, who showed it to Olybrius. Ricimer took action and named Olybrius emperor. That was in April, three months before the murder of Anthemius. On 11 July, just after the death of Anthemius, Olybrius officially became emperor. Ricimer and Olybrius did not have long to enjoy their successful coup. Ricimer died in August, possibly of tuberculosis, considering that the sources report that he had vomited up a great deal of blood. A severe case of dropsy ended the life of Olybrius.

John of Antioch, Fragment 209
Chronica Minora I, p. 306

LEO I
c. 401–18 January 474
Emperor of the Eastern Roman Empire from 7 February 457

LEO II
c. 467–17 November 474
Emperor of the Eastern Roman Empire from 18 January 474

While emperors in the west were succeeding one another at a rapid pace, in Constantinople Leo sat securely on the throne. On 18 January 457, following the death of Marcian, he received the imperial necklace in the royal box of the Hippodrome and was officially crowned in the Hagia Sophia by the patriarch of Constantinople. From then on he not only governed the east, but also kept a close eye on the situation in the west. Nevertheless his reign was not as trouble-free as its length – almost seventeen years – might cause one to suppose. He constantly had to be on the alert for sneak attacks from Goths and Vandals. His foreign policy was fairly successful, though his fleet did meet an inglorious defeat at the hands of the Vandals in north Africa. But his position was also undermined several times by internal threats. He had to deal with pretenders to the throne, especially in the years 466 to 471. Aspar, a general of Alan birth who had also served under Marcian, had been the emperor's trusted friend and confidant for years. But following a coup by his son Ardabur, which he probably knew more about than he let on, Aspar fell from grace and was eventually murdered, along with a large number of sympathisers. It must have been a particularly brutal crackdown, since the action earned Leo the nickname 'the Butcher'. It is doubtful if the incident caused him much sorrow. He had never been popular and wanted to use his authority to command respect, not affection.

No details are known about Leo's death. All we know from the sources is that he died of dysentery at the age of seventy-three. He was succeeded by his seven-year-old grandson Leo II, the son of his daughter Ariadne and her husband Zeno. Five months before his death Leo had picked him as his successor. Why he passed over his son-in-law, who had earned his spurs, and chose a child is not known. In the end things turned out well for Zeno: at the insistence of his mother, Leo II appointed his father co-regent three weeks after taking office. Nine months later the child emperor died, shortly after coming down with an unknown illness, and Zeno became the sole ruler. He remained emperor till his death in 491. From a distance he witnessed the disintegration of the Western Roman Empire.

Chronica Minora I, p. 307
Cedrenus 1.614.18

GLYCERIUS
?–after 474, perhaps 480
Emperor of the Western Roman Empire from
3/5 March 473 to June 474

Nine months before his death, Leo I was informed that another emperor had been appointed in Rome: Glycerius, put forward by Gundobad, who thought he could follow in the footsteps of his uncle Ricimer. The elderly Leo saw little in the newcomer, about whom we know nothing more than the fact that he had been a high-ranking magistrate and a general in Dalmatia. He sent an army with Julius Nepos at its head to Italy to depose Glycerius. It took some time, however, before Nepos took any real action. In the meantime Glycerius was reasonably successful in battling the Ostrogoths, who were threatening to invade Italy. This did not help him, however. In June 474 Nepos' fleet sailed into the harbour of Ostia. He succeeded in capturing Rome with little fighting. Glycerius was taken prisoner and stripped of his imperial decorations. And then Nepos did the same thing that Ricimer had done with Avitus: he appointed him bishop, in this case of Salonae in Dalmatia, the region he himself was from.

Jordanes, *Getica* 45.239–241
Anonymus Valesianus 7.36
John of Antioch, Fragment 209

NEPOS
?–480
Emperor of the Western Roman Empire from
19/24 June 474 to 28 August 475
Attempted to seize power again in May/June 480

But the story of Glycerius does not end there. Nepos became the new emperor, with the blessing of Zeno in Constantinople. There is no information about what he did over the course of the next several months. It seems he devoted most of his energies to fighting the Visigoths in Gaul. The spring of 475 heralded the fall of Nepos. One of his close advisers, Orestes, who boasted of having been the personal secretary of Attila the Hun, turned against him and won the support of the army. In Ravenna he proclaimed his son Romulus emperor. Nepos capitulated and fled to Dalmatia. There he reportedly made Glycerius his 'personal bishop'. It is unknown how much longer Glycerius lived after that. Perhaps he died in the same year as Nepos, 480. The circumstances under which Nepos met his end are not entirely clear. In Dalmatia he continued to act as if he were emperor and was recognised as such by Zeno. He had never given up the hope of one day returning to the highest office in the land. In 480, when his successor Romulus Augustulus was long gone from the political stage, he apparently made one last bid for power. But his followers had lost confidence in him and stabbed him to death on 22 June 480.

John of Antioch, Fragment 209
Anonymus Valesianus 7.36
Jordanes, *Historia Romana* 338–339
Getica 45.241

ROMULUS AUGUSTULUS
461–well after 476
Emperor of the Western Roman Empire from
31 October 475 to 31 August 476

The end of the Western Roman Empire, which had been looming for a few decades, was clearly in sight after 474. It is a strange twist of fate that the last emperor bore the name of Romulus, the founder of Rome. It is even more ironic that he has gone down in history as Augustulus ('little Augustus'). He was just fourteen years old when he became emperor and completely lacked the authority needed to maintain control of the armies. The problems with the soldiers escalated over the course of 476, when German mercenaries belonging to the tribes of the Heruli, the Scirii and the Rugii demanded land. Orestes, who assisted his young son in many areas, refused to grant this request. The soldiers then turned to Odoacer, an army captain of Scirian descent with Hun blood in his veins. He promised them land. They rewarded him for this by proclaiming him king on 23 August 476. Five days later Orestes was captured not far from Piacenza and killed. Romulus Augustulus retreated, probably to Ravenna, and anxiously awaited Odoacer's arrival. What he expected did not come to pass. Odoacer showed his compassionate side and spared the life of the youthful emperor, touched by his young age. Because Romulus Augustulus was prepared to write the Senate an official letter confirming his abdication, Odoacer promised him an annual pension of six thousand solidi, approximately the annual income of a senator. He lived for many years as a private citizen on a country estate in Campania. It would appear that he lived a carefree life there, though following Odoacer's death he did have to negotiate his yearly allowance with the Ostrogoth Theoderic, who had overthrown Odoacer. He took the position that he had never made any arrangements with him about a pension. But even if Theoderic had denied his request, we should not feel sorry for Romulus Augustulus; if anyone deserves our pity, it is Odoacer, who, thirteen years after being named king of the Germans in Italy, was betrayed and murdered.

Anonymus Valesianus 8.38
Jordanes, *Getica* 46.242

12

THE END OF ANTIQUITY

It has often been asked whether the dethronement of Romulus Augustulus should be seen as the formal end of the Roman Empire. In fact not a lot changed that year in Italy and western Europe. It is doubtful if the average inhabitant of Italy and western Europe even noticed the transfer of power. In the context of this book on the deaths of the Roman emperors, the year 476 was definitely a turning point, because the emperors of the west disappeared and were replaced by kings of German principalities. This is not to say, however, that people in Italy gave up the hope of renewed ties with the east for good. The myth of the Roman Empire lived on into the fifth and sixth centuries. The emperor in Constantinople was the link to the glorious Roman past, even for the German kings who succeeded the insurgent Odoacer. Right after deposing Romulus Augustulus, Odoacer accepted the title 'king' and recognised Zeno, the emperor of the Eastern Roman Empire, as the one true ruler.

Between 480 and 490 it became clear just how vulnerable and dependent his position was. Zeno was greatly troubled by the presence of marauding Ostrogoths in the Balkans. Afraid to raise taxes to improve and enlarge the army, he came up with another solution. He bought off the Ostrogoths and sent them to Italy to depose Odoacer. After several years of fighting, Theoderic, the king of the Ostrogoths, succeeded in overthrowing Odoacer by an act of treachery. In this way the Byzantine Empire easily resolved its Goth problem, and in 489 Italy became the kingdom of the Ostrogoths.

Under Theoderic, Italy experienced a final revival. From his headquarters in Ravenna he reigned as a sort of sub-emperor, the second man after the Eastern Roman emperor Anastasius. This new kingdom adopted a great deal from the Romans: the tax system, the currency, the administration and the system of patronage. In order to obtain co-operation from the old aristocratic Roman families,

Theoderic left the Senate intact, and with the permission of the emperor of the east, every year he would appoint Roman aristocrats consul. However, this never led to full integration. It remained a system of dual government, in which the Ostrogoths oversaw the Gothic part of the population and Roman magistrates the Roman part.

The kingdom of the Ostrogoths was of short duration. After Theoderic's death the Roman senators appealed to the then-emperor of Constantinople, Justinian (527–565), to liberate Italy. This request fitted in nicely with Justinian's plan to restore the Roman Empire. First his general Belisarius conquered north Africa, where he brought down the kingdom of the Vandals in 534. The army subsequently crossed over to Italy. Sicily was quickly subdued, but it was not until 557 that the whole of Italy was under Justinian's authority. To facilitate the administration of Italy the emperor appointed a governor, who ruled in his name.

Justinian's campaign of conquest was the last active attempt by an Eastern Roman emperor to regain control of the west. In 568, shortly after it was reunited with the east under Justinian, Italy was overwhelmed by the Lombards, a Germanic people from central Germany. The Roman authority now disappeared for good, and the Senate no longer functioned. In its place came dukes and counts, who governed the various districts; officially they did so in the name of the king, but in reality they had great personal power.

The Eastern Roman Empire continued to exist as the Byzantine Empire. The hope for reunification with the west never died out completely. In the seventh century, however, any real reason for hope faded: the Avars, a Slavic people from central Europe, occupied the Balkans and cut off the connecting roads to Italy. The Byzantines were not given time to repair them, because in the same century the Arabs took Egypt, Asia Minor and north Africa from the Byzantine Empire. When they also conquered Spain in 711 and began their domination of the Mediterranean Sea, all contacts between east and west were permanently broken.

FAMILY TREE 1 The Julio-Claudian Emperors

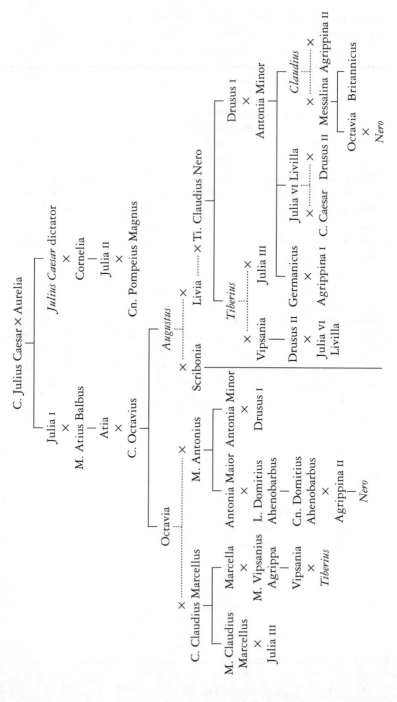

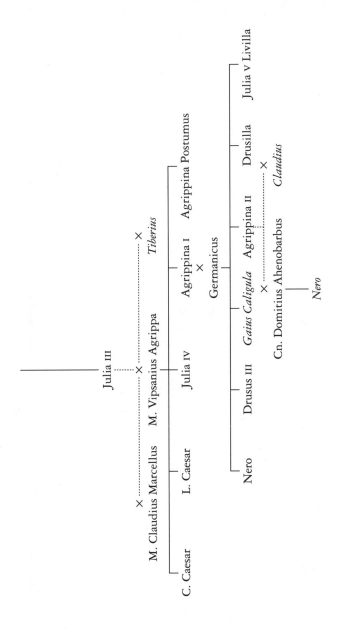

FAMILY TREE 2 The Antonine Emperors

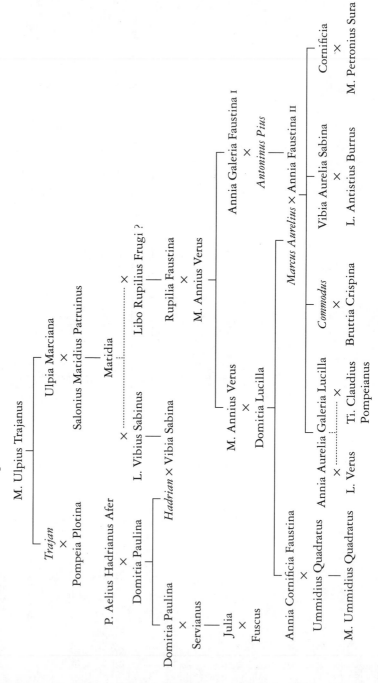

FAMILY TREE 3 The Dynasty of Septimius Severus

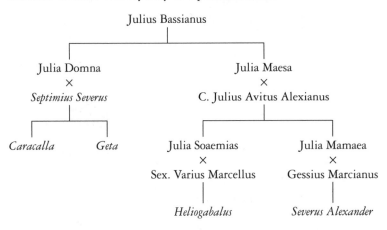

FAMILY TREE 4 The Dynasty of Constantine

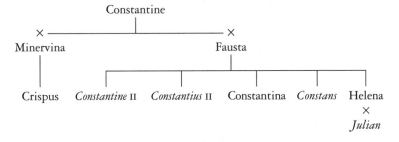

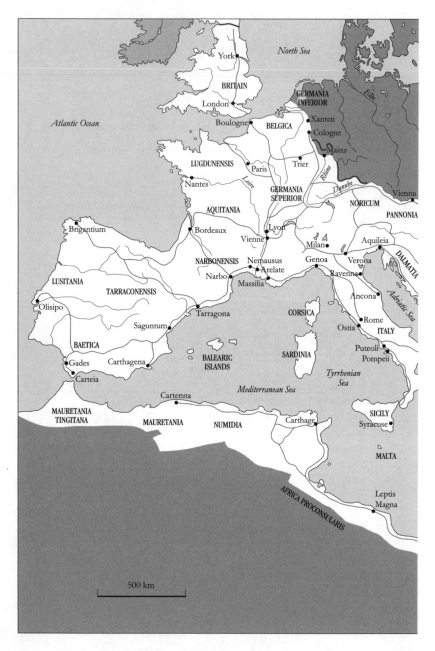

Map 1 The Roman Empire in the middle of the second century.

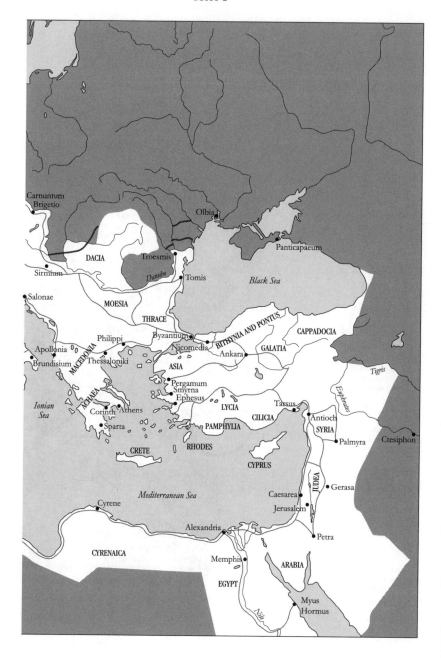

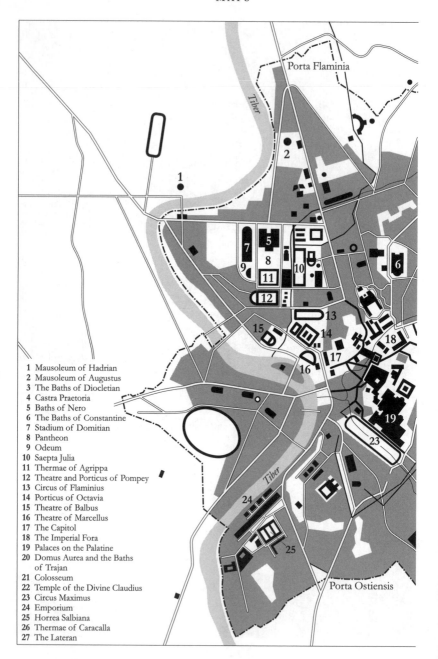

1 Mausoleum of Hadrian
2 Mausoleum of Augustus
3 The Baths of Diocletian
4 Castra Praetoria
5 Baths of Nero
6 The Baths of Constantine
7 Stadium of Domitian
8 Pantheon
9 Odeum
10 Saepta Julia
11 Thermae of Agrippa
12 Theatre and Porticus of Pompey
13 Circus of Flaminius
14 Porticus of Octavia
15 Theatre of Balbus
16 Theatre of Marcellus
17 The Capitol
18 The Imperial Fora
19 Palaces on the Palatine
20 Domus Aurea and the Baths
  of Trajan
21 Colosseum
22 Temple of the Divine Claudius
23 Circus Maximus
24 Emporium
25 Horrea Salbiana
26 Thermae of Caracalla
27 The Lateran

Map 2 Rome.

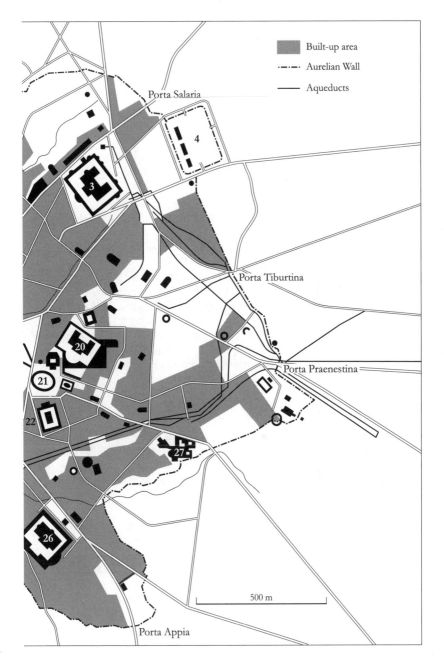

Built-up area

Aurelian Wall

Aqueducts

Porta Salaria

4

3

Porta Tiburtina

20

21

22

Porta Praenestina

27

26

500 m

Porta Appia

BIBLIOGRAPHY

I have taken a great deal of general information from the following works.

The new edition of *The Cambridge Ancient History*, published by L.E.S. Edwards (*et al.*), Cambridge 1961–2001.

Scarre, Chris (1995) *Chronicle of the Roman Emperors: The Reign-by-Reign Record of the Rulers of Imperial Rome*, London: Thames and Hudson.

Wissowa, G. and Kroll, W. (eds) (1894–1978) *Paulys Realencyclopädie der Classischen Altertumswissenschaft*, Stuttgart.

Ziegler, K. and Sontheimer, W. (eds) (1964–1975) *Der kleine Pauly: Lexicon der Antike*, Munich: Deutscher Taschenbuch Verlag.

Also useful was the online imperial chronicle *De Imperatoribus Romanis: An Online Encyclopedia of Roman Emperors* (http://www.roman-emperors.org).

Specialised literature

Arand, T. (2002) *Das schmähliche Ende: der Tod des schlechten Kaisers und seine literarische Gestaltung in der römischen Historiographie*, Frankfurt am Main: Peter Lang.

Balsdon, J.P.V.D. (1934) *The Emperor Gaius*, Oxford: Clarendon.

Barnes, T.D. (1981) *Constantine and Eusebius*, Cambridge, MA: Harvard University Press.

—— (1993) *Athanasius and Constantius: Theology and Politics in the Constantinian Empire*, Cambridge, MA: Harvard University Press.

Barrett, A.A. (1989) *Caligula: the Corruption of Power*, New Haven: Batsford.

—— (1996) *Agrippina: Sex, Power and Politics in the Early Empire*, New Haven: Yale University Press.

Bengston, H. (1979) *Die Flavier: Vespasian, Titus, Domitian*, Munich: Beck.

Bennett, J. (1997) *Trajan Optimus Princeps: A Life and Times*, London: Routledge.

Bidez, J. (1930) *La vie de l'empereur Julien*, Paris: Les Belles Lettres.

Birley, A. (1966) *Marcus Aurelius*, London: Batsford.

—— (1988) *The African Emperor: Septimius Severus*, London: Batsford.

Birley, A.R. (1997) *Hadrian: The Restless Emperor*, London: Routledge.

Blois, L. de (1976) *The Policy of the Emperor Galienus*, Leiden: Brill.

Brauer, G.C. (1975) *The Age of the Soldier Emperors: Imperial Rome, AD 244–288*, Park Ridge, NY: Noyes Press.

Browning, R. (1976) *The Emperor Julian*, Berkeley, Los Angeles: University of California Press.

Bury, J.B. (1958) *History of the Later Roman Empire from the Death of Theodosius I to the Death of Justinian*, New York: Dover Publications.

Cameron, A. (1993) *The Later Roman Empire*, Hammersmith, London: Fontana Press.

—— (1993) *The Mediterranean World in Late Antiquity AD 395–600*, London, New York: Routledge.

Cicatrix, J. and Rowson, M. (1995) *Imperial Exits*, London: Macmillan.

Cizek, E. (1994) *L'Empereur Aurélien et son temps*, Paris: Les Belles Lettres.

Demandt, A. (1997) *Das Privatleben der römischen Kaiser*, Munich: Beck.

Earl, D. (1968) *The Age of Augustus*, London: Elek.

Garzetti, A. (1974) *From Tiberius to the Antonines: A History of the Roman Empire, AD 14–192*, London: Methuen.

Grant, M. (1979) *Caesar*, London: Weidenfeld and Nicolson.

—— (1996) *The Severans: The Changed Roman Empire*, London: Routledge.

Greenhalgh, P.A.L. (1975) *The Year of the Four Emperors*, London: Weidenfeld and Nicolson.

Griffin, N. (1985) *Nero: The End of a Dynasty*, New Haven: Yale University Press.

Jones, A.H.M. (1964) *The Later Roman Empire, 284–602: A Social, Economic and Administrative Survey*, Oxford: Blackwell.

—— (1966) *The Decline of the Ancient World*, London: Longman.

—— (1977) *Augustus*, London: Chatto and Windus.

Jones, B.W. (1984) *The Emperor Titus*, London: Croon Helm.

—— (1992) *The Emperor Domitian*, London: Routledge.

Kienast, D. (1990) *Römische Kaisertabelle: Grundzüge einer römischen Kaiserchronologie*, Darmstadt: Wissenschaftliche Buchgesellschaft.

Levick, B. (1976) *Tiberius the Politician*, London: Batsford.

—— (1990) *Claudius*, New Haven: Yale University Press.

Meier, C. (1982) *Caesar*, Berlin: Severin and Siedler.

Millar, F. (1992) *The Emperor in the Roman World*, London: Duckworth.

Murison, C. (1992) *Suetonius: Galba, Otho, Vitellius*, Bristol: Bristol Classical Press.

Parker, H.M. (1969) *A History of the Roman World, AD 138–337*, London: Methuen.

Perowne, S. (1986) *Hadrian*, London: Routledge.

Pohlsander, H.A. (1996) *The Emperor Constantine*, London, New York: Routledge.

Scramuzza, V.M. (1940) *The Emperor Claudius*, Cambridge, MA: Harvard University Press.

Seeck, O. (1897–1920) *Geschichte des Untergangs der antiken Welt*, vols. I–VI, Berlin, Stuttgart.

Shotter, D.C. (1992) *Tiberius Caesar*, London: Routledge.

Southern, P. (1997) *Domitian: Tragic Tyrant*, London: Routledge.

—— (1998) *Augustus*, London: Routledge.

—— (2001) *The Roman Empire from Severus to Constantine*, London: Routledge.

Starr, C. (1982) *The Roman Empire 27 BC–AD 476: A Study in Survival*, New York, Oxford: Oxford University Press.

Warmington, B.H. (1969) *Nero: Reality and Legend*, London: Chatto and Windus.

Wellesley, K. (1989) *The Long Year AD 69*, Bristol: Bristol Classics Press.

Williams, S. (1985) *Diocletian and the Roman Recovery*, London: Batsford.

Wolfram, H. (1987) *History of the Goths*, Berkeley, Los Angeles: University of California Press.

INDEX

175